Christmas, 2012

This book was written by the Director/Founder of Matthew 25 Ministries, Rev. Wendell Mettey, a good friend of ours. At a Christmas luncheon they had for the volunteers, he introduced several (more than 50) who were chosen to be "pictures" of the characters he wrote about.

We didn't know anything about it until they revealed which volunteers were being pictured (by an artist who drew from the photographs provided.

Four of the "models" were volunteers from First Baptist Hamilton - 3 men & 1 woman. The 4 are shown on pages 26, 28, 47, & 95. You should be able to recognize Simeon & Anna (pages 26 & 28)!!

After we got our copy, and read those 2 articles, I decided to go back and get a copy for each of our sons. This is for your whole family - and we'd like to to know that everyone in the family will take the time to read it (the whole book). We were honored to be chosen to represent Simeon and Anna!

Love, Mom & Dad

MEET THOSE WHO MET THE MASTER

MEET
THOSE
WHO MET
THE MASTER

By Rev. Wendell E. Mettey

MEET THOSE WHO MET THE MASTER

Copyright © 2012 by Reverend Wendell E. Mettey

All direct quotes made by Jesus or other characters are taken
from the Holy Bible, NEW INTERNATIONAL VERSION®.

Copyright © 1973, 1978, 1984 by Biblica, Inc.
All rights reserved worldwide. Used with permission.

ISBN-10: 0985834013
ISBN-13: 978-0-9858340-1-2

Book Website
m25m.org/theleastofthese
bookstore@m25m.org

Give feedback on the book at
bookstore@m25m.org

Cover Design: Lauren Kelly

Printed in U.S.A.

TABLE OF CONTENTS

TABLE OF CONTENTS

ACKNOWLEDGEMENTS

I thank Joodi Archer for her endless hours of editing, countless hours of research and all the hours of administrative work that went on behind the scenes, especially taking all the photographs of each character. I thank all of our staff and volunteers for being such good sports when we singled them out to have their pictures taken and for allowing us to drape them with scarves and pose them to get just the right "look." I'd like to thank Larry Keller who brought each character to life with his remarkable artistic talent and Reverend David Palmer, PhD who has the heart of a pastor, the mind of a scholar and who gave me much insight into first century Palestine. I'd like to thank my wife, Mickey, for typing the original document and for serving as the "definitive" editor, my son, Tim Mettey, for his project management on this book and my staff members Karen Otto, Lauren Kelly and Lori Harding for their assistance with research, typing and scanning. It has taken many hands to bring this book to life and I dedicate the final product to all those who have worked so hard for so long on this project.

A WORD ABOUT THE CHARACTERS YOU WILL MEET

Will Rogers, the famous humorist once said long before the twenty-four-hour cable news channels, "All I know is what I read in the newspaper."

Most of what we know about the people mentioned in the Gospels is what we read in the Gospels: a name, a description, an illness, a confrontation. Then, as quickly as they appear, they disappear, never to be seen or heard of again.

Naturally the Gospel writers had to limit their stories. John says it best, "Jesus did many other things as well. If every one of them were written down, I suppose that even the whole world would not have room for the books that would be written." *John 21:25*

Perhaps there is another reason we are told so little about these people we meet ever so briefly. It raises our curiosity and, in order to satisfy our curiosity, we must go beyond what we are told and ask questions.

Take, for example, John the Forerunner. We are told more about John than most you will meet, yet we are told very little. We know Mary and Elizabeth were relatives. We know that Mary visited Elizabeth when they were both pregnant.

Does this mean that Jesus and John grew up together? They lived eighty miles apart, a significant distance in that time. How often did they see one another? Jesus grew up in the village of Nazareth in a northern area called Galilee. John lived south in the hills of Judea, practically growing up in the wilderness. Were one or both influenced by the Essenes who had withdrawn into the desert to live in simplicity and purity and to usher in the coming of the Messiah? The wilderness was their home and they lived near Qumran. Here the Dead Sea Scrolls were discovered by a shepherd boy in 1947.

Other characters, other questions. Mary Magdalene is mentioned in Luke 8 as a follower of Jesus "from whom seven demons had gone out." *Luke 8:2* Is she the sinful woman mentioned in Luke 7 who washed Jesus' feet with her tears and hair and anointed Him with oil? Many think so. Then there's Jairus; the thankful leper; Zacchaeus; Martha; the woman bleeding; the widow of Nain; the would-be disciple; the paralytic; the rich ruler and so on…

I have attempted to bring these people to life and to share their experience of meeting the Master, not through mere speculation, but by relying upon the best evidence available: the four Gospels, Bible scholars, early Church fathers and tradition as well as my own understanding of human nature. I am always asking the question, "What would I do in their situation?" Lastly, I have relied heavily upon my understanding of how God works with people.

While two thousand years have brought about considerable change in the world, I believe the struggles, concerns and ultimate questions which faced the individuals of the first century are still the same issues that you and I face in the twenty-first century. Hopefully, in reading how these individuals came to meet the Master, we might also meet Him or, perhaps, meet the Master in a new and powerful way.

CHARACTER DEVELOPMENT

The development of each character is based on the scriptural passages listed at the beginning of each chapter. I would encourage you to go to your Bible and read Luke's original description of the character and the incident prior to reading the expanded stories in this book. This will give you a firm Biblical foundation to work from when experiencing characters who may have been enhanced by "sanctified imagination."

USING ALL AVAILABLE INFORMATION

While most of the characters you will meet are mentioned, referred to, or actually appear in the Gospel of Luke, many also appear in the other three Gospels, especially the Gospel of Matthew. I will often use the information from the other Gospels in order to give more detail to the characters' lives and to fill out Luke's text where necessary. For example, after Jesus was born, Luke implies that the holy family went straight to the city of Nazareth in the district of Galilee. In Matthew, the holy family seeks to escape the murderous wrath of Herod by fleeing Bethlehem and traveling to Egypt, which was outside of Herod's jurisdiction. They stay there for a couple of years. The angel then tells Joseph that it is safe to return, but that they will live in Galilee in a town called Nazareth. Luke has the holy family going straight home and Matthew has them detouring through Egypt and then home.

The stories are not mutually exclusive and there are several possible reasons for the differences. Perhaps Luke knew about the flight into Egypt but simply chose not to use it. Perhaps, since Luke's Gospel is based on stories and character studies, Luke was not aware of the flight into Egypt because no one shared that information with him. Or, perhaps Luke was responding to the guidance of the Holy Spirit, who directed each author in their choices about what God desired each to write. Luke's words, "When Joseph and Mary had done everything required by the Law of the Lord, they returned to Galilee to their own town of Nazareth" *Luke 2:39* and the comment "and Jesus grew in wisdom and stature, and in favor with God and man" *Luke 2:52* suggest that he may have employed a form of literary compression to move more quickly to Jesus' next appearance on the stage of history. In this context, the phrase "done everything required by the Law of the Lord" could be inclusive of their time spent in Egypt at God's command.

In Elizabeth's story, she speaks of Mary visiting her upon her return from Egypt. The length of the route between Egypt and Nazareth (more than 200 miles) makes it plausible that Mary and Joseph would have stopped to visit with Elizabeth and Zechariah in Judea, especially given their affection for one another. Mary and Joseph's flight into Egypt and their subsequent return was foretold in Hosea 11:1 "When Israel was a child, I loved him, and out of Egypt I called my son."

I have attempted to be historically accurate regarding the ages of all the characters, which posed real challenges, taking into consideration the life span in the first century compared to that of the twenty-first century. I used the final time that each character spoke as a way of determining the current age of the character within a story. For example, when Elizabeth gave birth to John, she could have been in her 40s or 50s. Some thirty years later, she talks to Jesus, who was at that time 31-34 years of age, suggesting that she was at least in her 70s at the time of that conversation. Mary was probably in her teens when she had Jesus and was also present at the cross, making her, at that time, possibly in her mid-40s.

I have used historical data and research from biblical scholars to create characters and situations that are as fully-formed as possible within the context of what would have been plausible during that time period.

ABOUT THE ILLUSTRATIONS

All of the drawings, with the exception of the thief on the cross, are the faces of either volunteers or staff members at Matthew 25: Ministries. Each day for an entire summer, we walked through our 132,000 square foot warehouse looking for interesting faces that would represent the people who met the Master. It was a labor of love, and a labor intended to emphasize the distinctiveness of the people we discovered. We used a collection of scarves to create a semblance of the period, but our main focus was on the personality and character of the person and less on costumes and make-up. We got what we wanted: a collection of ordinary people doing extraordinary things through Matthew 25: Ministries... the same types of ordinary people who thousands of years ago met the Master and were called by Him to do extraordinary things. The artist, Larry Keller, is self-taught and discovered the joy of art and painting in elementary school. Larry attended the University of Cincinnati and retired as a senior project engineer after forty years at Ford Motor Company. Larry produced 1–2 character sketches a day for Reverend Mettey's book. He and his wife, Marilyn, live in Milford, OH.

A GREAT DISCOVERY

Reading the Bible is a great adventure, filled with many wonderful and unexpected discoveries. Each time I open the Bible I discover something new. That's what happened to me when I began reading the Gospel of Luke.

Have you had the opportunity to meet the man who wrote not only the Gospel of Luke but also the Book of Acts? He's only mentioned three times in the entire New Testament, all by the Apostle Paul. We learn from Paul's letter to the Colossians that Luke is a medical doctor. Paul refers to him as "Our dear friend Luke, the doctor." *Colossians 4:14* In another letter, Paul requests that his young friend Timothy come to him because all had left him, except for Luke. Paul writes, "Only Luke is with me." *II Timothy 4:11* Finally, in his letter to a man named Philemon, Paul calls Luke his "fellow worker." *Philemon 1:24*

We are given so little information and, yet, we are told a great deal. Luke was a faithful and loyal friend to Paul. He stayed by Paul's side to the very end of Paul's life. He was a committed worker for the Lord and the Church. He was also a person who had given his life to healing. He was an exceptional man.

Tradition tells us that Luke was a Gentile who received his medical training in Tarsus, which was a famous center for learning. It was also the home of the Apostle Paul. As circumstance would have it, or I should say as Providence made possible, it was Luke who came to care for an ailing Paul. Perhaps their conversation about Tarsus led Paul to share why he was far from home, and he then introduced the beloved physician, Luke, to Jesus Christ. In meeting Paul, Luke met the Master.

After Paul was executed in Rome about AD 67, Luke took it upon himself to write an orderly account of the life of Jesus Christ and the story of the growth and development of the early Church. After doing extensive research, with much of the information coming from eye-witnesses, Luke compiled two books: Luke, the third Gospel and carrier of his name, and Acts, or Acts of the Apostles, a history of the early Christian community.

Back to the discovery.

While I was reading Luke's Gospel I found myself counting. No, not the pages or chapters of the book, but the people Luke mentioned in his Gospel, either by name or description; people Luke identified as individuals who met Jesus face-to-face. By my count, at story's end, there were over ninety identified individuals, in addition to those who were with those identified and the thousands more who were in the crowds and synagogues where Jesus taught.

Interesting… more than interesting… a great discovery! I thought I knew Luke's Gospel from cover-to-cover. I had read it, studied it, preached it and taught it for years, yet I had not noticed that Luke tells his story through people. Not just any people, *but those who met Jesus, face-to-face*.

Quite logical, I thought. Who else could better tell the story than those who had a personal encounter with Jesus. Who else could tell what Jesus was like, each relating a different experience, each revealing another dimension of His life. They were there. It happened to them.

Then something fascinating happened. One-by-one, they stepped out of Luke's Gospel and spoke to me of their experiences with the Master. Some stories were inspiring, others comforting. Still others were challenging, and many disturbing. Yet when all had had their say, I felt I had met the Master anew.

I invite you now to come along with me and Meet Those Who Met the Master.

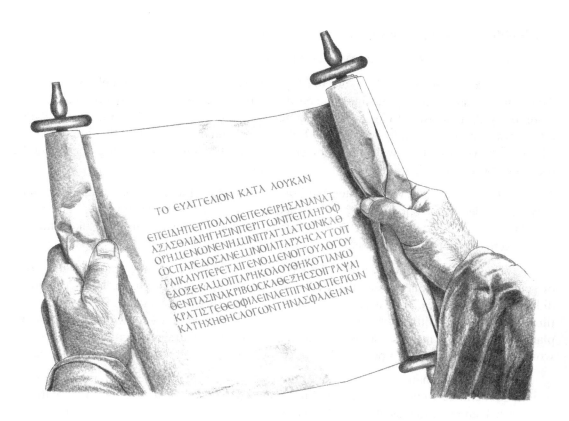

Theophilus

Lover of God

Luke 1:1-4

I must say… many of you have been most creative in your attempts to identify me. Some of you have maintained that my parents believed in the pantheon of the Greek and Roman gods, but converted to Judaism about the time I was born. They gave me the name Theophilus, which means, "One who loves God." It was a common name both to the Greeks and Hebrews. You may have assumed that I observed the sacred festivals with my parents, especially Passover, however, I was not a believer. I found religion unchallenging, bogged down by archaic rules, myths and folklore. I much preferred politics to religion. It was exhilarating wielding so much power... the display of wealth… the control over other people's lives. Notice how Luke greeted me as "Most Excellent" *Luke 1:3*… a tribute to my high social status and an acknowledgement of my patronage.

There has always been interest in how Luke and I met. Why did he dedicate his two books to me… a man of the world, a man of law, not love? Let me tell you. I was visiting the outer provinces of Phoenicia and North Galilee when I came down with malaria. The doctor who they called to my side was Luke. He stayed with me for weeks, skillfully caring for me and eventually restoring me to full health. After Luke would examine me he would lay his hands on me, bow his head and whisper something I couldn't quite hear. One day, I asked what he was doing and saying. He said he was praying that I would be healed. He then told me that when the Master laid His hands on the ill, they became well and when He touched the hopeless or downhearted, they were given the strength to face any difficulty.

I asked him, "Who is this 'Master' of yours?"

That question unleashed a torrent of questions and answers which took us well into the morning. I asked many questions and contested many points, but eventually I had nothing more to say. At that point, Luke said I had better get some rest, to which I responded, "REST? I don't want to rest, I want to hear more!" Luke smiled and said softly that the time for talking was over. I must now decide whether to give my life to the Master or go on living the way I had been… as a good man but not God's man.

"I want to accept your Master, but I don't know how. Please, Luke, please show me how!" I pleaded. Luke laid his hands on me and there in that tent far from home, I accepted the Master as my Lord and Savior. So, I met and accepted the Master through Luke, although I never actually met Him in person.

That's right! I'm not like any of the people you are about to meet, but I am like all of you… for you, also, never met the Master face-to-face. Oh, I could have. The occasions did present themselves, but I was always too busy… affairs of state and all. Besides, at that time the Master was little more than a mere curiosity to me; certainly not worth changing my plans or rearranging my busy schedule. Then, after the physician read his manuscript to me, I would have given away all I possessed to have met Him as did those you are about to meet.

To touch the hands which cleansed the lepers, gave sight to the blind, made the lame walk…. to be there when He fed that enormous crowd… five thousand, some say… with just two fish and five loaves of bread, little more than a boy's lunch. Amazing! To have heard Him summon forth Lazarus from the tomb… to have sat on that hillside and heard Him teach, "Blessed are the poor in spirit, for theirs is the kingdom of heaven… blessed are the meek… the merciful… the peacemakers…" *Matthew 5:3-12* To have seen Him walk on water and quiet an angry sea… to be in that upper room and have heard Him say to His deeply troubled disciples, "Do not let your hearts be troubled. You believe in God; believe also in me." *John 14:1* Then, to have stood at the empty tomb when on that day, God raised Him from the grave… Oh, what I would have given… to… to… um, yes, where was I? Oh, yes…

What I want to tell you is this: it is not too late. I had to meet the Master through another, and now so can you. If it had not been for Luke, I would never have met Jesus at all. Luke not only told me of the Master, but because the Master lived in Luke, I met the Master as vividly and personally as anyone could… and so can you.

I would imagine there are many people in your time, as I was in mine, who have never met Him or who know so little about Him. The only way they will meet Him is to meet Him through someone else… maybe you.

There are many Theophiluses. May they all find a Luke to help them meet the Master.

"Oh Master, lead me to that one today whom I may lead to you… Amen."

Elizabeth

Dear Cousin

Luke 1:5-25, 39-80

"Zechariah! Zechariah, it's Mary and Joseph."

What a joyous surprise. Our cousins, our dearest friends had finally come back from their exile in Egypt. The words of the prophet Hosea came to me, "I chose to bring my son out of Egypt." *Hosea 11:1* Later that day, Joseph told us he was guided throughout their long trek by dreams. In his fourth and final dream, Joseph was warned not to go back to Bethlehem. The cruel and ruthless King Archelaus ruled there in place of his dead father, Herod the Great. Archelaus killed 3,000 people while celebrating Passover during his first days in office! Joseph was told to go north to Galilee and live in their hometown of Nazareth. Instead of going straight home, they paid us a wonderful visit.

Oh my, how long had it been since we saw each other? I was five, no, six months pregnant with John when Mary journeyed eighty miles to tell me she was also pregnant. Yes, now I remember… when I heard Mary's voice, the baby in my womb leaped for joy. The Holy Spirit came over me and I said to Mary with a loud voice, "Blessed are you among women, and blessed is the child you will bear!" *Luke 1:42*

Then my sweet, sweet Mary began to sing, "My soul glorifies the Lord and my spirit rejoices in God my Savior… from now on all generations will call me blessed." *Luke 1:46-48*

It is remarkable to look back on those days and reflect on how differently things might have gone. Mary and I talked about it during her visit. "Who would have believed it?" she asked. "A virgin with child... why would Joseph believe me? He is an honorable and generous man... but this?" How blessed she was that Joseph took her to be wed anyway. Our society was not forgiving to unmarried women who were pregnant. Yet in our tradition every life matters to God, unlike the pagan practices of the Romans, who used a mixture of poison herbs to kill an unwanted child in the womb, or left the newborn exposed on a hillside, condemning it to death. How marvelous it was that Joseph trusted in God and saved Mary and Jesus from a similar fate!

Mary and her family stayed with us for three months and then went home to Nazareth.

My husband Zechariah and I had waited a long time for a child of our own. Both of us were advanced in years. Zechariah was a priest belonging to the priestly division of Abijah; both of us were from the tribe of Levi. We followed the Law blamelessly, but because we were childless, people pointed their fingers and wagged their tongues when we passed, saying we must have in some way lost favor with God. The town gossip didn't stop until I held my child in my arms, a son Zechariah named John, which means "the Lord is gracious." Our son "grew and became strong in spirit." *Luke 1:80* No one could ask for a better son.

After my dear Zechariah died, John came to me one evening. I was arranging flowers outside Zechariah's tomb. He told me what his father and I had long suspected. He said that he would not follow in the priestly footsteps of his father. No, God had called him to be a prophet. Then he spoke the words of Isaiah. Holding my hands he said, "I am the voice of one calling in the wilderness, 'Prepare the way for the Lord, make straight paths for him.' Every valley shall be filled in, every mountain and hill made low. The crooked roads shall become straight, the rough ways smooth. And all people will see God's salvation." *Luke 3:4-6*

God had called John to preach "a baptism of repentance for the forgiveness of sins." *Luke 3:3* I was so proud of him, yet so afraid. When the people heard John, they came in droves; seeking forgiveness for their sins and baptism by John in the River Jordan at a place called Salim, near a heavily travelled trade route. John told the people that it didn't matter if they were poor peasants, wealthy merchants, high ranking soldiers, or even the High Priest... they needed to repent and receive God's forgiveness... everyone must be ready for the arrival of the King. I was glad that He was doing God's work, but also concerned. He was beginning to direct his message at some powerful individuals... even Herod Antipas himself.

Then it happened. John publicly called for Herod Antipas to give up his sinful relationship with his brother Philip's wife, Herodias. Herod, son of Herod the Great, feared John because of his popularity with the people and so he had John arrested and put into the fortress of Machaerus near the shore of the Dead Sea. But Herodias, that temptress, hated John and tricked Herod into killing... him. That day my life ended. My grief was overwhelming. I asked God daily to take my life. Someone told me that when Jesus heard about John's death, His sorrow was so great He got into a boat all alone and went to a solitary place to pray and to grieve deeply for John, His dear cousin, a prophet and the forerunner for Jesus.

Overcome with grief, I had a friend take me to Nazareth. Such a long journey, but I needed to be with Mary. Sitting one evening, first with Mary, then alone, I met the Master. No longer a boy of three, nor a teenager who had spent summers with us, nor even the young man who stood by His mother when His father, Joseph, died. No, He was now the Master.

He was so gentle and compassionate. He came to me in my darkest hour of despair. The burning fires of bitterness raging within me were extinguished by His soothing words. "Why Jesus, why," I sobbed, "would God wait so long to give us a son, and then take him away so quickly? Was this God's will?"

He told me this was an important and necessary part of God's eternal plan. He spoke to me of matters of which I was unaware. He said that God had a greater plan and that John and Zechariah both played an important part in that plan, and that I did too. But why me, I asked Him, so old and helpless. How? He said I was chosen to be John's mother and now, chosen to give comfort and wisdom to His mother, Mary. As He spoke, my faith and trust in God was gradually restored. I shall never forget what His parting words to me were: He told me that Zechariah and John lived in Him.

When He asked me if I believed Him, I answered unwaveringly, looking into His eyes, "Yes, Master, I do." And I did because it was no ordinary man who spoke those words. It was the Master and I met Him that night.

"Master, come to me each day and help me see your plan for my life... Amen."

Mary

Can He Be the One?

Luke 1:26-56, 2:1-20

At the time, I thought of myself as a typical mother. However, I felt our son was anything but typical. Yet, to say we knew He was special, well, doesn't every mother feel that way about her children? James, Joseph, Judas, and Simon, Jesus' four brothers and His sisters, they were special in their own way. But Jesus, well, the moment Joseph placed Him in my arms in that Bethlehem stable, I whispered, "Can He be the one?"

I didn't feel special, but I knew deep in my heart that what Joseph and I were asked to do was special. I have pondered these words for over thirty years: "My soul glorifies the Lord and my spirit rejoices in God my Savior... for the Mighty One has done great things for me... He has lifted up the humble... He has filled the hungry with good things..." *Luke 1:46-53* But there is always that lingering question, why were we chosen? A young, ordinary handmaiden and a carpenter?

The one thing I ask of you is to remember that you've had over two thousand years to make sense of all of this. We had but a few years. Things happened that were beyond our understanding. This explains why we acted the way we did. Even though the angels told us and it seems so clear to you, well, you'd have to go through it for yourself to know what I mean. That is to say, don't judge us too harshly for the things we did. We were only human.

Like mothers do, I constantly worried about Jesus, especially when He began His public ministry and started speaking about His "Heavenly Father." The crowds who were following Him kept getting larger and larger. Even then, I freely gave Him my motherly advice and asked Him for favors. I felt I had a right because after all, I was His mother. He was never disrespectful. However, on several occasions He reminded me that God's desires must come first. On one occasion, I was simply crushed. I went to see Him, and when His disciples told Him that His mother and His brothers were there to see Him, He said, "Here are my mother and my brothers. For whoever does the will of my Father in heaven is my brother and sister and mother." *Matthew 12:49-50*

In time I realized that I could not protect Him or change things. If I had my way He'd still be my little boy playing in His father's workshop. But that would have been selfish. I have those years etched in my memory forever. Memory is such a precious gift, especially when times are difficult and lonely.

Simeon's prophecy spoken over thirty years ago kept going around and around in my mind: "This child is destined to cause the falling and rising of many in Israel, and to be a sign that will be spoken against, so that the thoughts of many hearts will be revealed. And a sword will pierce your own soul too." *Luke 2:34-35* After Herod had imprisoned and murdered John, those words never left me.

I did not always do what was best for Jesus, nor did His brothers and sisters. My concern for His safety blinded me. His brothers did not believe Jesus was anything more than their flesh and blood brother, especially James. On one occasion, they tempted Jesus to prove He was who He claimed to be. They told Him to leave safe Galilee and go to Jerusalem where the people weren't so easily fooled. "Show yourself to the world," they said. *John 7:4*

One day, things came to a breaking point. People told us He was saying He was the Son of God. The entire family went to find Him. We thought the pressure was getting to Him. We found Him and physically pulled Him aside. We told Him people were saying His words were blasphemous, dangerous. Things had gotten out of hand and we were going to take Him back to Nazareth. He rebuked all of us and walked away with His followers.

Now I understand His behavior. His hour was upon Him. Satan fought Him at every turn. His journey was difficult and the temptations were many. He did not need us to line up behind the Evil One with our well-meaning but misguided intentions. He needed our support. He needed those who would help Him do His Father's will. I could see that now.

That was when I had to stop being just a mother. I had been honored above all women to carry within my womb the Son of God; to hold Him that first miraculous night; to hear the words of the angels; to raise Him and watch Him grow into a man; to see Him become the Master. But I could no longer be just His mother. I had to start being, with all the others, a disciple.

"Master, help me to love you as did Mary and to follow you as your disciple...Amen."

Joseph

A Model for Fathers

Luke 2:1-20, 2:41-52

Did I meet the Master? I was His father! Well, not really His father; a guardian. That's how I thought of myself. Jesus had but one Father, His heavenly Father. As close as I was to Jesus, He was closer to Abba Father, as He often referred to His heavenly Father.

This deep abiding relationship our son had with God was first revealed to us in a frightening, yet powerful way one time in Jerusalem. Every male Jew, once they turned twelve, was privileged to travel to Jerusalem for the three great feasts of Passover, Pentecost and Tabernacles. That year, we had gone to the Holy City for Passover. We were gone from Jerusalem about a day when we looked around for Jesus but could not find Him. We were traveling with a large group of family and friends and we assumed He was with other family members. His mother was beside herself. He was only twelve years old and could be lost in a very big city. We both vividly remembered that horrible night shortly after his birth when Herod the Great had every male child under the age of two murdered. Led by a dream, we miraculously escaped that bloodbath.

After searching everywhere, we returned to Jerusalem. We finally found Him after a couple of days. We were so relieved to find Him that we did not notice what was taking place. We rushed into the gathering, crashing the party, so to speak. We were not warmly welcomed. On the contrary! "Quiet!" the crowd shouted. "Leave the boy alone. Let Him speak!" One man stood up, pointed at us and shouted, "Who are these people?" Mary responded indignantly, "We are His parents!" The man sat down and once again all became quiet. They were waiting for my son to speak! One of the men, a chief elder and leading teacher, said softly as he stared at Jesus, "You have an amazing son. We have never heard such wisdom!"

Walking from the Temple we scolded Him for going off on His own and not telling us. He responded, simply but without apology that He had to go about His Father's business. Nothing could be more important than that. He was the best son any parent could ask for. But He was our adopted son. We hadn't adopted Him. God adopted us to bring His Son into the world and care for Him until He became a man… His Man. Ever so slowly He became less and less ours and more and more His! We were gradually losing Him. On that day in Jerusalem it began.

It is difficult to let go of someone you love, especially your children. You care for them, protect them. There is nothing you wouldn't do for your children. And then the time comes when they must leave and be on their own. If they are to follow their calling and take their place in the service of God this must happen. We had to let go, knowing that our son, as no other son or daughter, would be called upon to save an entire world! The prophets spoke of what He must endure for all that to take place. We, too, prayed to His heavenly Father to watch over our son, His Son, who was now the Master.

"Oh Master, may my relationship with the heavenly Father grow in strength and love. To know you as Jesus did… Amen."

Simeon

A Long Wait Rewarded

Luke 2:21-35

Have you ever had a religious experience? I mean, maybe… perhaps… a dream of some kind? I don't know what you might call it. Call it what you will, it was a wonderful, yet frightening, experience.

There was a bright light and these words, "Behold, Simeon, you will see the Messiah born in your lifetime. You will bless Him and hold Him in your arms." That was it, nothing more... just those words. As quickly as they came they were gone.

A long time has passed since that experience, almost a lifetime. I have waited and watched for the child in a thousand faces. I have questioned countless pilgrims coming in and out of the temple, but no Messiah. And how would I recognize Him? Who should I be looking for? A child? A warrior who would drive the Romans from our land? A prophet who would comfort His people? A ruler who would bring peace to all people?

After sixty years of waiting, I simply could not get out of bed. I was too old, too tired. Someone else… someone younger than I was must keep watch. The vision was all but a faded memory now. That was it… it was only a dream. Young men are famous for having dreams. Suddenly, there before me was that light again. After all these years, it reappeared. This time just two words were spoken twice. "This day. This day." I managed to find the strength to get up and walk to the temple. Could this be the day for which I had waited? Such a long time to wait. But it would all be worth it to behold the Messiah.

Again I faced the problem: so many people. How would I recognize Him? All day I searched. Finally I sat down, wondering if I had somehow missed Him. As I was preparing to leave the temple, a couple approached me carrying a child. I told them they would have to find another to dedicate their child. I could not. I was too tired. I was waiting for someone. As they walked away, a strange feeling came over me. "Wait! Wait," I shouted. How foolish could I be! "Where was your child born?" I asked. "Bethlehem," they answered. "His name?" I asked. "Jesus," they whispered. I took Him into my arms. "This is the Messiah," I proclaimed to all around us. I began to sing, "Sovereign Lord, as you have promised, you may now dismiss your servant in peace. For my eyes have seen your salvation, which you have prepared in the sight of all nations: a light for revelation to the Gentiles, and the glory of your people Israel." *Luke 2:29-32*

I took the couple to a quiet place. I told them of the vision I had. I then told them what was told to me, that "This child is destined to cause the falling and rising of many in Israel, and to be a sign that will be spoken against, so that the thoughts of many hearts will be revealed. And a sword will pierce your own soul too." *Luke 2:34-35* I prayed with them, blessed their child and sent them on their way. God answers all prayers. Praise God I had met the Master.

"Master, may my faith stand the test of time. May I always watch for your coming... Amen."

Anna

A Life Given to Serving God

Luke 2:36-40

Simeon is my good friend… you remember… the man you met yesterday. Well, I too had a spiritual experience of sorts when I was young. I did not have a vision like Simeon. No, mine was a still, small voice. It whispered one day: "Anna, you have been anointed with the gift of prophecy." God had placed within my heart a sensitivity which enabled me to see in others their potential for good or evil.

As the daughter of Phanuel out of the tribe of Asher, I was betrothed to a man of my tribe. It was prearranged while we were young. We married. We had no children. Seven years of marriage ended when my husband died. He was a dear and kind man. I miss him terribly. Now I had a decision to make: marry another, or follow the still, small voice and use my gift of prophecy. In accordance with the Law, I announced my desire to serve God and His Temple. I'm eighty-four years old now. I have served God faithfully, seldom leaving the Temple. Fasting and praying has brought to me an even greater gift of prophecy. Kings and beggars, they all have come to me seeking my words of prophecy.

One day my old friend, Simeon, came to me carrying a child, shouting like an old fool, "This is He! This is He! Anna, I tell you, He is the one." A large crowd gathered around us. "Here," he said, "Confirm my vision. Tell me who this is."

I held the boy in my arms. I knew at once. I shouted, "The Messiah! The Messiah! Simeon, God has fulfilled your vision. You have seen Him." I, too, held the baby above my head. With outstretched arms, again I shouted, "The hope of the world!" The people cheered. They did not understand. They thought it was merely the custom of hope. Every male child had the potential of being the Messiah. I carried the child to a quiet place. His parents and Simeon stood around me.

I looked at them. They both looked bewildered. What I sensed in their son's life deeply saddened me, yet brought wondrous joy. "His life will end so that ours will not. Be strong and know your child belongs to the entire world." I gave them back their child. Standing next to Simeon, we watched them walk from the Temple. We had met the Master. Our faithfulness had been rewarded.

"Master, show me how to serve you with joy and faithfulness and discover the gift within me... Amen."

Teacher

My Father's Business

Luke 2:41-52

We were utterly amazed. He had such wisdom… such knowledge… and was so, so young. Rabbis from all over Israel had gathered in Jerusalem for Passover. He listened to them and spoke to them with such maturity and depth of understanding. He was mesmerizing. He quoted the Torah from memory. He answered one question after another without hesitation and with great clarity and insight. Judging from the weave of His clothing and His dialect, He certainly was from the North, perhaps from one of the small villages near the Sea of Galilee. But can that much learning be obtained in such a rural setting? What wisdom could be taught by a small-town Rabbi in some remote synagogue? No, while His parents and Rabbi obviously taught Him well, such learning can only come from God.

Some of the Rabbis and Pharisees said His words were revolutionary, others said they bordered on blasphemy. When they could not refute His interpretations of the Law, they'd just smile and, with a condescending attitude, try to dismiss the boy by changing topics. But those gathered there wanted to hear from the boy, telling the others to sit down or leave.

He was a handsome child, and respectful. He had a most pleasant demeanor. He had a playful sense of humor and knew when and where to use it. He taught by telling stories, which everyone could grasp.

While He was speaking, a woman was circulating through the crowd, saying she had been healed at the Pool of Bethesda, a spring-fed pool that was supposed to possess healing virtues. This caused quite a stir. Where she was healed was not the issue; the issue was that she was healed on the Sabbath. According to the Law of Moses, there could be no change in any object (including a person's physical status) on the Sabbath. Veins bulging in their necks, the Pharisees pronounced that the healing was a blasphemy… that there were six other days on which she could have gone to the pool to be healed.

The boy spoke up and with a remarkable authority questioned why a daughter of Abraham should endure her pain and agony for one more day? He pointed out that we untie our animals to give them hay and water on the Sabbath. Why should we do less for this woman? He said that the Sabbath was given by God to benefit man, not to make man a slave of the Sabbath.

Just as that topic was going to be hotly debated, His mother and father came to get Him. Apparently, the boy didn't tell His parents of His plans to stay behind. For days they had looked for Him. The mother said, "Son, why have you treated us like this? Your father and I have been anxiously searching for you," *Luke 2:48* and He replied, "Didn't you know I had to be in my Father's house?" *Luke 2:49* What did that mean? As they were leaving, I walked to the mother and said, "This child will always be God's man!"

The day before His parents came, I was concerned for His welfare, so I invited Him to stay in my home nearby. I gave Him some lamb and unleavened bread leftover from Passover. Just a child of twelve years, yet I began pouring out my worries and troubles. I had grown cynical. Too often I had seen the worst of men. I was even questioning my faith, my belief in a God who could possibly still love such a miserable world. He put His hand on my shoulder and said the strangest, yet most comforting words, that God loved all the world with such depth, that He'd sacrifice His own son to save it.

Eighteen years later, I was on that mount in Galilee when He preached to the crowds. I was also there when he fed the multitude with a few fish and loaves of bread. He was no longer a twelve-year-old boy, but a man with a powerful message of God's steadfast love for all peoples and forgiveness for even those who persecuted us. I had met the Master, and He made me whole.

"Oh God, when our problems become so complicated and overwhelming, may we remember the simple words of our faith told to us by the Master… Amen."

Caiaphas, the High Priest

A Caustic Heart

Luke 3:1-2

Most of you don't like me very much. Many of you downright despise me. If I may speak in my own defense, being the High Priest at that time was no easy job. It was a balancing act. We had to deal with the Romans, who conquered and ruled us with an iron fist. However, because our religion was fully formed when Rome was still an undeveloped swamp, the Romans allowed us to continue practicing our own religion and did not compel us to worship Caesar, unlike their other occupied people. As long as we kept the peace and paid our taxes, there was no trouble. However, Israel has a long history of revolting against any people who sought to occupy them. Soon, I fear, there will be another revolt and mighty Rome will crush us.

Take, for example, this group of fanatics called the Zealots. From their point of view, there was no compromise. The Romans must go, by the sword, if necessary. They prayed fervently for a warrior Messiah who would come with a sword and drive out the foreign occupiers.

Trying to keep them all from each other's throats and at the same time run the Temple... well, let's just say it was challenging. Now don't get me wrong. There were certain benefits and privileges that came with the calling. What I'm trying to say is, it wasn't easy; but I will have to admit, it was a gratifying position.

Oh, did I mention the Pharisees, the "Experts in the Law?" They were rigorous in their application of the Torah. They wanted what the Romans had... control. This is where your Master got in trouble.

We tried to keep things sailing along as smoothly as possible. We didn't need anyone rocking the boat. We didn't need anyone stirring things up by trying to reinterpret our religion. And we certainly didn't need a prophet like John running around saying that Herod was committing adultery by living with his brother's wife. So let him live with his brother's wife, as long as it keeps him occupied. Personally, I didn't want John to die. We respected John. Also, he was rather amusing. He gave us something to break the monotony of this place. But he was dangerous because he was so blunt.

I have seen more than my share of those Zealots come and go in my lifetime. The world they talk about is not real... it is just some philosophical fantasy. The only reality is what you can see in front of you and what I see is the Roman might. If you cooperate, you are given a few crumbs. If you don't, well, ask John or that Master of yours what happens.

And concerning this Master of yours, yes, I'll admit it. I did say before the Sanhedrin it was better that one man die for the people than the whole nation perish. We knew He must die when He supposedly raised Lazarus from the grave (that was just too flashy), and I did plot with the others to kill Him. It was for the best. We were attracting too much notice. We were about to lose our "crumbs."

I didn't have to do too much. He managed to get the elders in the Sanhedrin all riled up without much help from me. Not only did His own people not recognize Him, they crucified Him. And just look at His followers: Trash! Prostitutes! Beggars! Low lifes! A few women and some misguided Galileans. Bah!

Yes, I met the Master. I must say, out of the bunch of fanatics that I have seen pass through here, He was the most impressive. He wasn't your ordinary run-of-the-mill lunatic. There was something hypnotic, mystifying about Him.

Yes, I met your Master. I was impressed, yes, impressed, but not convinced. God will have to do better.

"Master, keep me from becoming callous and cynical, from being trapped and fooled by the trappings of this world... Amen."

Forty Days and Forty Nights

An Epic Battle

Luke 4:1-13

I remember when I finally broke my silence… when I spoke for the very first time of the events I had witnessed so long ago in that vast, cold, empty desert. Empty, that is, except for Him… and His tormenter.

"Doctor Luke! Doctor Luke, a few minutes of your time. Could we go over to the shade of those trees? Well, um…" I stuttered. "I've, well, been practicing what I'd say… but now I don't know where to begin."

"Doctor, I heard you are writing a gospel… the good news of the life of the Master, Jesus the Christ. I've also heard that many people are stepping forward, some at great personal risk and telling how they met the Master. I wish to do the same. As far as I know, I am the only eyewitness to this frightening yet truly astonishing experience. I haven't told anyone about this these many years. Why? People would say I was mad. Here's my story… judge me as you will."

☙ ❧

My story begins at a fork in the road. I was passing through the Judean wilderness. Do you know it? It's a massive stretch of land over five hundred square miles. It's cradled by the Dead Sea and stretches all the way to the hills of Judea. This is truly a place of devastation… uninhabitable… a place where people go seeking refuge from their enemies or escape from life's concerns.

At this particular fork in the road, I could go north and take the safer road around the great wilderness, or I could choose the other road (actually just a path) and go up and through the wilderness, shortening my journey home by three days. Since I had travelled this path before, I decided to go through the wilderness. The path winds through a sea of stones, all sizes and shapes. It is notorious for its jagged outcrops of gigantic boulders and deep chasms lining the treacherous path. The hills are surrounded by limestone cliffs and thousands of caves cut out of the soft sandstone.

Many hours later, I arrived at the Bethlehem plateau, a place flat and free of stones, and a good place to spend the night. Needing water, I climbed down to the nearest wadi and filled my pouches. On the way back, I saw something emanating from the plateau, some kind of light which I had never seen before. I could see colors of reds, yellows and oranges. There was a heavy fog covering the entire area. Although there was a full moon, a thick layer of clouds hid its light. It was pitch dark except for this eerie light coming from the plateau. I crept forward, and hid behind a large rock. Peeking around the rock, I could make out two figures: two men in white robes. One man looked tired and weak, sitting on a large stone, His head buried in His hands. He was clearly exhausted and in great anguish. The other figure was much larger; he stood a considerable height and constantly waved his arms as he circled the tired man. Each time it seemed that he was going to touch the man, a noise filled the air. To me, it was a most beautiful sound, like a chorus of angels. Just then, the larger figure would cover his ears and retreat. The noise seemed to have some power over him.

The large figure then commanded with a seductive voice, "If you are the Son of God, tell this stone to become a loaf of bread." *Luke 4:3*

I thought, *Yes, Lord! Then we could feed the hungry!*

The man answered, "It is written man does not live by bread alone." *Luke 4:4*

Oh, my God! At that moment, I knew who these figures were… the one was Beelzebub… Satan… the Prince of Demons… the Devil… and the other was Jesus the Rabbi from Nazareth. Undeterred, the Prince of Demons conjured up a vision of all the kingdoms of the world and grandly declared, "I will give you all their authority and splendor; it has been given to me, and I can give it to anyone I want to." *Luke 4:6-7*

Jesus answered, "It is written: 'Worship the Lord your God and serve Him only.'" *Luke 4:8* Finally, Beelzebub transformed the plateau into the Temple in Jerusalem and took Jesus to the highest point of the Temple.

From that dizzying height, he yelled at Him, "If you are the Son of God, throw yourself down from here. For it is written: 'He will command his angels concerning you to guard you carefully; they will lift you up in their hands, so that you will not strike your foot against a stone.'" *Luke 4:9-11*

Jesus answered, "It is also said: 'Do not put the Lord your God to the test.'" *Luke 4:12*

With those words, Satan was defeated and left; the young Rabbi fell to the ground. I ran to His side, lifted up His head to give Him water. He asked what month and day it was.

"Why, it is the tenth of Shevat," I answered. He then accepted some water, saying that His forty day fast was over. I was astonished! No food or water for forty days in the wilderness! No wonder He had seemed so tired and weak. He said He had to go. I gave Him some food and water for His trip home and then He left. As I walked away, I thought of Psalm 91: "If you say, The Lord is my refuge, and you make the Most High your dwelling, no harm will overtake you, no disaster will come near your tent. For he will command his angels concerning you to guard you in all your ways; they will lift you up in their hands, so that you will not strike your foot against a stone." *Psalm 91:9-12*

"Am I mad, good Doctor?" I asked. "Can I possibly have been witness to such a monumental struggle between good and evil?" Luke said no, I was not mad, but blessed. I witnessed firsthand the power of Satan and the greater power of God. He also said to me that a retelling of this story would be in the book he was writing so all would know the power of the Devil and the greater power of God.

"Lord, grant me the strength and steadfastness of spirit the Master demonstrated when confronted with temptation... Amen"

John the Forerunner

A Call to Repent

Luke 3:2-22, 7:18-33

I speak to you from the prison of Machaerus, one of Herod's fortresses. My preaching apparently struck home. Herod came to see me in secret, pleading for my silence. "Forgive me," he begged. I replied, "Rid yourself of your brother's wife and plead with God, not with me, for forgiveness."

As I'm sure my mother has told you, I met Jesus when I was three. His family had just returned from Egypt. We spent many summers together growing up. Unlike most children, we talked about God and the part we were to play in His divine plan. As mentioned, we journeyed often into the wilderness and even visited a group of isolated people called the Essenes. They had left Jerusalem because it had become so corrupt. They emphasized simple living and the need for repentance and practiced water baptism. They had a tremendous influence on my life. My mother commented that I practically lived there. I only wore camel's hair clothes and a leather belt around my waist. I ate nothing but wild honey and locusts. I depended on God for all my needs.

As my mother said, one day the spirit and words of the prophet Isaiah came over me. I burst from the wilderness preaching a message of repentance. I told... no, I warned them to flee from the wrath to come. "The ax is already at the root of the trees." *Luke 3:9*

"Repent and be baptized," I preached.

Sometime later, I was baptizing in the Jordan River. Many came to repent their sins, receive forgiveness and be baptized. People came from all over Judea and Galilee. Then one day Jesus stepped from the crowd. I could not speak because I knew the time all creation had awaited was about to begin. After expressing my feeling of unworthiness in baptizing Him, I did… but only after He insisted. Little did I know then I would not see Him again... and I didn't.

As my mother told you, Herod had me arrested and put in prison. From behind these bars I speak to you. I must tell you I was so discouraged. I felt my life was a failure. There are so many I did not reach. Such doubt I had. Was Jesus really the one? I sent one of my disciples to find Jesus and ask Him, "Are you the one?"

What did He say? Jesus told my disciple, "Go back and report to John what you have seen and heard: the blind receive sight, the lame walk, those who have leprosy are cleansed, the deaf hear, the dead are raised, and the good news is proclaimed to the poor. Blessed is anyone who does not stumble on account of me." *Luke 7:22-23*

Jesus then turned to the crowd and said this about John: "What did you go out into the wilderness to see? A reed swayed by the wind? If not, what did you go out to see? A man dressed in fine clothes? No, those who wear expensive clothes and indulge in luxury are in palaces. But what did you go out to see? A prophet? Yes, I tell you, and more than a prophet. This is the one about whom it is written… I will send my messenger ahead of you, who will prepare your way before you. I tell you, among those born of women there is no one greater than John; yet the one who is least in the kingdom of God is greater than he." *Luke 7:24-28*

When His words reached me, I was so joyful. It was told to me that He must increase while I decrease. My time in the wilderness with Jesus has prepared me for this moment. If I hadn't met the Master, I would not have been able to bear the evil around me, or face so calmly what waits for me. But I have met Him, and because of that I have the strength to carry me through whatever the morning may bring.

"To know you Master as John did. Visit me, Lord, when I am a captive... Amen."

Simon's Mother-in-Law

Saved to Serve

Luke 4:38-39

Did you notice that the physician Luke does not call me by my name? I have one, you know. You might think this oversight would upset me, make me feel unappreciated. You would be right… until a few years ago. That is when I met the Master.

I don't know who did the inviting, but someone special… the talk of Galilee… was coming to our home. As Simon's mother-in-law, that meant I would do all the work and everyone else would have all the fun. But to tell you the truth, I'd have it no other way. While I wanted to take part… well, I felt uncomfortable around a lot of people. I always felt inadequate. So I stayed in the shadows of others and worked behind the scenes. Good old what's-her-name… oh yeah, Simon's mother-in-law.

All day before the Sabbath I worked getting things ready for our company. That morning, I started feeling poorly. I hadn't slept the night before and I was beginning to feel feverish. I thought it was just the heat, nothing to be concerned about. *I'll be sick tomorrow; it's not in my schedule today.* By late afternoon I had to lie down. I was running a high fever.

I began drifting in and out of a deep sleep. My family took on distorted shapes as they huddled around me. Someone wiped my face with a damp cloth. They loosened my clothes. Their voices became distant and I began to hallucinate. I dreamed I was in quicksand... slowly sinking out of sight. I tried but could not reach my family. My family attempted to pull me free but they could not reach me. It was no use. I would surely sink to the bottom and die. No one could save me.

Suddenly, I saw a face. Then a hand stretched out towards me. I reached up and grabbed it. With a firm grip of my hand I was pulled from the sand. I then heard a voice calling my name... over and over... I was no longer afraid... I had never felt so much love before. A peace came over me. I felt needed...

I felt saved... not to serve men, but to serve God. I woke up. I heard voices, happy voices saying that I was alright, praising and thanking God. The face I saw smiling at me... it was the Master. He was the one who saved me.

My family tried to make me stay in bed. But I insisted on getting up. "No, I'll wait on you," I declared. Now when I wait on others, I'm waiting on the Lord because I have met the Master.

"Oh Master, help me see that all I do is done for you. Help me accept myself and rejoice greatly... Amen."

Simon Called Peter

The Reluctant Disciple

Luke 5:1-11

It was a hot summer's evening. I needed to get out of the house and find a cool breeze. I also needed to clear my head. Things were going too fast. First the Master dined at my house at the invitation of my brother Andrew. I was told nothing about it! Then my wife's mother became ill and miraculously the Rabbi healed her. *This isn't for me. I am a fisherman. I don't want to get mixed up in any trouble. I just want to fish!* I listened to them inside my house laughing and having a good time. I don't think any of them understood what He wanted from us or the cost of following Him.

Someone put a hand on my shoulder. It was Jesus. How could I know He was not like all the other false Prophets, the so-called Messiahs? They were after self-glory, power, or even worse, they were chasing an unrealistic dream. The only thing I understood was a net full of fish.

We sat down. With great passion He talked about setting men and women free from sin, about bringing help to those in need and light to those living in darkness. He told me that we don't live by bread alone. I was impressed but did not want to make a commitment.

He asked me if I had heard what happened to Him in His home town of Nazareth. "I heard they rejected you," I answered. He then asked me why this happened. I told Him it was His interpretation of the book of Isaiah… or so people said. It had been the talk of Galilee.

He asked me if I could quote the words from Isaiah. "Yes, since I was a child," I replied and proceeded to do so. "The Spirit of the Sovereign Lord is on me, because the Lord has anointed me to proclaim good news to the poor. He has sent me to bind up the brokenhearted, to proclaim freedom for the captives and release from darkness for the prisoners, to proclaim the year of the Lord's favor." *Isaiah 61:1-2* The Master smiled. He then said that was why He came into the world. He said He was asking others to come and help Him.

A few days later, I had come in from a disappointing day of fishing. I was cleaning the boat and repairing my nets when a large crowd of people came to the shoreline. A few approached me asking permission for the Rabbi to use my boat. I agreed, with some reservations. After climbing into the boat, I rowed Him back out onto the lake.

He spoke to the crowd about things I had never heard before. I felt a pull on my life... but again I held back. Then He called to me and my partners to go out into deep water and for us to lower our nets. Reluctantly, we did as He said. Unbelievable! We caught so many fish it almost capsized our boats. The Master said for us not to be afraid, that we would henceforth "fish for people." *Luke 5:10* At that moment, I accepted Him and committed to follow Him no matter what. I could resist no longer. He was truly God's man. I had met the Master. I wanted the whole world to do the same.

"Oh Lord, in Simon I find a lot of me. Discipline my spirit, Master, that I may be counted on when called upon to give all to you. Give me daily bread but also the bread of life... Amen."

James

Fisherman Three

Luke 5:10

I'm James. My younger brother John and I used to work with our father. We were in the fishing business. Some years later we went in with Simon and his brother Andrew and formed a business partnership. We do all right. We work hard and our nets seldom come up empty. It was a good move, going in with Simon. Father was skeptical at first. He said that going into business with a friend was the best way to make him an enemy. But father was the first to admit he was wrong. We did not become enemies, but the best of friends.

Yes, I, too, remember that day, the one Simon just spoke to you about. The day I, also, met the Master. Unlike Simon and my brother John, I had never met the Master. Simon met Him at his house. John had met the Master on a number of occasions. When we were out fishing, John constantly talked about the Rabbi. The things John said, especially about the healings, were difficult to believe. We dismissed most of what he said as a young man's exaggeration. However, one thing came through: Jesus was like no other. He saw the world and God differently. He taught with great authority. He spoke of loving God with all we possess and loving our neighbor as ourselves. He taught us to love one another as He loved us… to the point of dying on a cross for us.

Then that day all I heard was what had happened at Simon's house. John went on and on. "Simon, is this true? Did He heal your wife's mother?" Simon didn't say a word, just nodded his head. "What do you make of Him, Simon?" I pressed. Again nothing, just a harder pull on the nets and a motion for me to do the same. John moved closer to Simon. Touching him on his shoulder, he said, "Simon, tell me, do you think He is the Messiah?" Simon dropped his net.

Looking up at the blue sky and the birds circling overhead, he spoke softly, "Oh, sinner that I am, do not ask me." John and I looked at one another. Simon was deeply moved. Something hidden deep within him had been brought to the surface by meeting the Master. We had never seen Simon like this before. Turning, his face twisted with anguish, he said, "First, daily bread. Then I will consider the Bread of Life." Simon returned to his nets. They were empty. You know the rest.

Why did I follow Simon and my brother in following the Master? It was impulsive, impetuous. To meet someone just one time and give up all to follow him. Well, I knew Simon, and for such a change to come over him, I knew it had to be the real thing. At first it was because of them—Simon and John. But when I saw what happened that day, I met the Master for myself. Sometimes a good thing comes along only once. You had better seize the day! I did. Will you?

"Master... when you knock... may I open the door before you move on... Amen."

The Man Full of Leprosy

Touched by God

Luke 5:12-16

I met the Master only one time. That one encounter not only cleansed my body, it changed my life. I was diagnosed with a form of leprosy called "the flesh eater" some years ago. In the beginning, it was just dry patches of skin, first on my arms then all over my body. My hands and limbs began to twist and bend. The disease doesn't stop until one is completely deformed. Our lives as lepers are regulated by Leviticus, a book of the Old Testament. We are the Untouchables.

It is difficult in your time to comprehend leprosy, to know the agony we went through. A disease, true, but to others, because of its hideous marks upon the flesh and the deformities, it was seen as a curse. The fear of catching it caused the Pharisees, using the Law, to regulate how we could live, where we could go, what we could do, even how we should die. We survived on table scraps thrown before us as if we were dogs. Alms? Guilt offerings? We were lower than the dogs that licked our wounds. There were those who brought help to us daily... clothes to wear and food to eat. They were God's angels.

The greatest pain, however, was the loneliness. Not even our families were permitted to be with us. We were the untouchables of society. People even believed that looking upon a leper could bring the curse upon them, so we lived in segregated colonies… in caves mostly… with no hygiene and filled with the stench of rotting flesh. We touched one another only to close the eyelids of those freed by death. As the disease worsened we had to rely completely upon others in the colonies even to put food into our mouths. We prayed for God's forgiveness of the sin which brought this curse upon us and for death which would release us from it.

One day I was walking outside of Capernaum. A large crowd came upon me. I quickly covered myself. Before I knew it I was surrounded. I heard someone mention the name of Jesus.

Jesus! I thought. My heart quickened with anticipation. It was my chance to be free from the curse. Here was the man who gave sight to the blind, healed the sick... surely He could heal me. I threw back my cloak exposing my leprosy. Everyone jumped back and covered their faces. "Master, if you will, cleanse me," I cried. Then for the first time in years, I felt the touch of another human being. The Master raised my head. He stretched out His hand and touched me again. I felt dizzy. My vision became blurry. I looked down at my arms, my legs. I was healed. The crowd began coming closer. One by one, they looked and then shouted, "He's healed! He's clean!"

"Praise God!" I screamed. I yelled, I danced...

The people were cheering and praising God. The Master then told me to go to the priest and have him confirm my healing according to the Law of Moses. Luke records that He told me to tell no one. That is true, but I, alone, know the meaning of those words. I was not to tell in words but to go and take what had happened that day, its meaning, to the others who sit in great darkness. He sent me as a messenger of hope... back to my fellow lepers. I could do this now because I had met the Master.

"Master, make me more sensitive to those around me who feel the helplessness of the leper. To do what I can to bring hope and wholeness to their lives... Amen."

The Paralytic

Dropped Through the Roof

Luke 5:17-26

I have been confined to bed for thousands upon thousands of days, only able to move the upper part of my body due to a foolish accident when I was just a boy. If it weren't for my dear friends (who never allowed me to give up during those long, painful, agonizing years), I would have been even more miserable and depressed; I would have found a way to end it all long ago. But my friends would not permit me to indulge in self-pity. They never gave up on me nor accepted that I was beyond help. They carried me to the Pool of Siloam, the Twelve Salt Springs, to one healer after another. I tried all types of herbs and potions. "This time," they said, as they had said so often before, "It will be different. We know you will be healed."

As we drew nearer to the house where the man from Galilee was staying, I could tell this was different. People like me, from all over Galilee, Samaria, and even as far away as Judea, stood in a long line to see the Rabbi. I have never seen such suffering, so much disease and illness. Some were walking on their own. Many were crawling on their hands and knees calling out, "Mercy, mercy, oh, Jesus, have mercy." There was no pushing or shoving; it was the blind helping the blind find a morsel of food. I was deeply touched by such compassion. My friends said to me that this was the teaching of the Master. That we should love and care for one another. My hopes were high… more so than at any other time.

The crowd was huge. I became discouraged that I would never get in, but my friends would not allow this obstacle to stand in the way of me seeing the Galilean. Determined, they hoisted me up on the roof of the house. After literally peeling away a section of the roof they lowered me with ropes through the hole, right into the middle of the room below. When I reached the floor everyone scattered and became silent. Jesus stood up. Smiling at me, He spoke, not of my healing, but of my sins being forgiven. An argument broke out among the other Rabbis present over whether Jesus had the authority to say my sins were forgiven. It seemed strange that they were more concerned with obeying the Law than making me whole.

The Master turned to me and told me to get up and walk. My mind rejected such an idea, but my entire body felt new life where there was none before. I lacked the courage to do as Jesus commanded. I looked up. My friends were coaxing me to get up; they kept motioning for me to try. For them, I tried, and because of the Master, I walked!

I met the Master. My sins were forgiven. My body was made whole. I met the Master because my friends cared enough to bring me to the one who loved people like me. I wish for you to have friends such as these and a healing Master such as the Galilean.

"Oh Lord and Master, thank you for friends who never give up on me even when I would give up on myself... Amen."

Levi Called Matthew

Wanting Nothing in Return

Luke 5:27-39

Did you know that I, Levi, the hated tax collector from the city of Capernaum, appear in the lineage of Jesus? My ancestor was the third son of Jacob and Leah. My tribe, the tribe of Levi, was praised for their faithfulness during the incident with the golden calf. *Exodus 32* But not me. Take what you can, as much as you can, from whom you can... that was my motto for living.

Then one day it happened. It was hot… dusty. People were paying their taxes, all the time muttering insults and threats under their breath. It was just business as usual… over the years, I had grown callous to such talk. "Next," I said.

The voice was soft, yet firm. Someone called me by name and said for me to walk not in the darkness, but in the light. I slowly looked up. Everything became quiet, muffled. Things seemed to move in slow motion. The sun was in my eyes. I squinted to see who spoke such words.

"Yes, I am Levi. Who are you?" I asked.

Again, the voice repeated that I was lost, but that God had found me. It said that although I was hated for what I do, that God loved me for who I am. I stood up and stared at the one before me.

"What do you want of me?" I asked.

The person before me said He wanted nothing from me except for me to receive God who loves me more than I know. He said that is why He came into the world, to free us from our sins. Then I knew who He was: the Rabbi from Nazareth.

"But, what do you want of me?" I pursued. "Everybody wants something. That's the way the game is played. There's always a payoff. What's the catch?"

The Rabbi smiled and said he had need of nothing from any man or woman. He said that His Father supplied all His needs. He told me the only thing He wanted for me was what His Father has to give us. He told me to claim the moment... to come follow Him.

And I did. To you, I made the right choice... I did the right thing. My tax collector friends thought I was crazy. Most would have nothing to do with me. What I did was a sign of weakness and could cause problems with the Romans. But that didn't matter now. I knew I was forgiven. I knew I had been lost but was now found. I was loved... truly loved for the first time in my life. I met the Master and He made me whole.

In His honor, I had a great banquet for the Master. I invited all my friends... most were tax collectors like myself. They kept asking all day if I were mad to give up my tax collecting table. Well, I wanted them to meet Jesus, so they could answer their own questions.

From across the street and through the open window, we could hear the Pharisees hurling insults at Jesus. "If you say you are a Rabbi, why do you eat with tax collectors and sinners?" they shouted.

When Jesus stood up, everyone inside my house got very quiet. Jesus walked to the doorway and said to the Pharisees that if they weren't sick, they didn't need a doctor, and if they were sinless, they didn't need to repent.

What could they say? They could not say they were without sin even though some of them acted as if they were sinless because they kept the Law. They made faces, turned and walked away. We then proceeded to have a wonderful party because all my friends met the Master.

"Master, I praise you for the persistent love you have for even those who feel and act unworthy of you, because Lord, that is often me... Amen."

Bartholomew

Leaders and Followers

Luke 6:12-16

Not counting the women who travelled with us, there were eighty-four followers… twelve He called apostles and seventy-two He designated as disciples. We followed Jesus wherever He went and were deeply committed to His teachings. One morning, after praying all night on the hillside, He called all of us together. From the eighty-four gathered, He designated seventy-two to be His disciples and sent them out two-by-two, warning them, "The harvest is plentiful, but the workers are few. Ask the Lord of the harvest, therefore, to send out workers into his harvest field. Go! I am sending you out like lambs among wolves. Do not take a purse or bag or sandals; and do not greet anyone on the road." *Luke 10:2-4*

Then from those remaining He chose twelve of us to be His apostles. The word in Greek means "one who is sent out to be a messenger." The twelve of us were the closest to the Master and we always had the feeling the Master was preparing us for something special. He also sent us out, telling us, "Take nothing for the journey… no staff, no bag, no bread, no money, no extra shirt. Whatever house you enter, stay there until you leave that town. If people do not welcome you, leave their town and shake the dust off your feet as a testimony against them." *Luke 9:3-5*

I felt honored to be chosen as did the others, yet there was something that always bothered me. Let me ask you, have you ever heard my name spoken first, before the names of the rest of Apostles? When the Apostles are listed, Peter (the rock) and Judas (the traitor) are always first and last. Then following are Andrew, James and John, Philip, Matthew, and Thomas…but where are James son of Alpheaus; Simon (Zealot); Judas son of James; Bartholomew, or Nathaniel, my other name. I'm always tucked away somewhere in the middle of a long list… never recognized in any way. In my time, one's place in a list indicated one's relative level of importance. So what did that make me? Unmemorable. Think about it, do you know of anything we did for which we are talked about?

In fact, we were like most of you. A few, like Peter, were chosen to lead but many, like me, were chosen to follow. At first that upset me, and the other five apostles would also agree. Most of the attention in the Gospel stories is given to Simon, his brother Andrew, the brothers James and John, Thomas who doubted Jesus' resurrection, and even Judas. Yet we were there also… the others… the ones needed to make up the twelve. But we never received special attention or consideration. I suppose you might say we were fortunate even to have our names included in such a group. Being a follower can be most unglamorous.

Then one day, the Master asked me to walk with Him down to the seashore. This was unusual. I could not remember any time when it was just the two of us. Simon, James, and John were often alone with Him… never Bartholomew! But the others had gone to their homes which were just a few miles away. Later I discovered that Jesus had arranged for this time together not only with me but also with the other overlooked apostles. Against the noise of the waves crashing on the shore, we talked of how the ministry was going. He talked with me about my family. He then told me a story.

It was about a man with twelve sons. Six of them seemed to consume most of his time. One was the eldest; he needed to talk about running the estate. Another was the youngest. Then there was the one always in trouble, and still two others who had great potential but much to learn. Finally there was one who grieved his father because of his rebellious nature. The other six sons were one with the father. They did all that the father asked. The father could always count on them. The time he had to give to the others was made possible by the time not required of him by these six sons. The father found joy in all of his sons (save the rebellious one) in different ways.

The years have passed and I now regret that my name is mentioned at all. The less attention the Master had to give to me, the more He had for the others and for His work. Now, that's not to say that my brother, Simon, wanted it that way, nor James or John, but they had been called to lead and I was called to follow. I was glad I could bring joy to the Master because He could always count on me.

"Oh Master, at times I too feel neglected and overlooked. Yet let me push those feelings away and serve you as a disciple who never causes you any bother… Amen."

The Centurion

A Matter of Faith

Luke 7:1-10

I must say, it puzzles me why the beloved physician would want to mention me in his story about the Master. There is nothing noteworthy about my story. My action, which I'm told brought praise from the Master, is what any good soldier would have done. Never question an order. I expected this of my men and they expected the same from me. When I said something had to be done, it was! Why did the Master equate my training as a soldier with faith?

Many of my predecessors hated the Judean tour of duty. To them, being stationed there was a demotion, a falling from Rome's favor. But I especially liked the people, and ever so cautiously, I came to believe in their God. Caesar was just a man and the gods of Rome just marble statues. But the God of the Hebrews, no, He doesn't act like the Roman gods do. He is unmoved by the trivial affairs of petty men. The God of the Hebrews, called Yahweh, is constant, He changes not. His ways are higher than our ways. His understanding far exceeded ours. He became my God… mine… a centurion in the Roman Army. How ironic!

So, I assisted the Judeans. I even helped build a synagogue, all in the name of keeping the taxpayers happy. That's the status Rome wanted. Happy people meant no revolts, which meant no taxes needed to be diverted to pay armies to keep the peace. This meant all the taxes could go to providing those in Rome, even some here in Judea, with a lavish lifestyle. Still, I had to be very careful, walking a thin tightrope between benevolent administrator and collaborator.

I lost many friends in battle, but when my beloved servant became ill, I can't explain it, but I could not bear the thought of losing him. Day-by-day his condition worsened. Did I dare tip my hand? Calling for the Galilean might be more than I could explain to Rome. It was one thing to be a great benefactor and builder of a synagogue, but it would be something else entirely to call for help from an itinerant Rabbi. Wouldn't it have been better to let my servant die than to show such disloyalty to Rome? I decided I had to take the chance. I sent for Him, and in doing so, I discovered why the Master spoke of my action as faith.

This was the first time I had turned to faith and stepped forward as a humble petitioner to the God of the Hebrews. Before, I had always accomplished things by might. The army that won did so because might was on its side. More soldiers, better weapons, wiser officers… might! That day I went against all my training as a soldier, but in this battle, I was helpless. The outcome was determined by something else… something small, yet powerful… faith.

It was not my rank that impressed the Master. It was me! An outsider, a conqueror, yet someone who went to God on faith alone, and He rewarded my faith by making my servant well. After my servant was healed, did I go to meet the Master? What do you think?

"Master, to risk it all for a friend. May I possess the faith and courage to do as this man did… Amen."

The Widow of Nain

A Son Raised

Luke 7:11-17

I'm from a little town in Galilee called Nain. You have probably never heard of it… few have. It is about a day's journey from Capernaum. It sits on a hill between Gilboa and Tabor. Its name means "delightful" or "pleasant."

The day I met the Master, my life was anything but pleasant. I was on my way to bury my son. I was now the childless widow of Nain. Since I had no protector, my possessions could be claimed by others. My husband's name would not be passed down. One day, I had it all… a husband who loved and cared for me, a son devoted to his mother… who could have asked for more? One day, I was somebody; the next I became a nobody, the widow of Nain. I lived at the complete mercy of the people of Nain. Unfair, you say, yes, but they had their families to care for. That day, I lived only for the moment when I would see my son and husband once again in heaven.

That day, while walking from the city, my friends wept for three: my husband, my son and for me. I wept not for myself, but for the men in my life, taken so early. Life was hard in my day. Many died young. It was an accepted reality of our lives. Yet we all carried the hope that we would live to see our grandchildren. For me that hope was gone. I did not even get to see my son take a wife.

Many have asked me why the Master stopped the funeral procession and raised my son. Surely He had passed other processions taking their dead to the tombs. "Why your son, on this day?" they asked. I have pondered this myself. Perhaps He was just moved by compassion, or perhaps He was overwhelmed at my grief. His purpose on earth was not to save us from death. No, He came so that we would have eternal life after we die. That is true. Yet, even the Master could not detach Himself from the feelings of others. So, He did what He did, because He was the man that He was.

But there was much more, I think. His action said something loud and clear… it had nothing to do with my husband or son being dead or alive. In His eyes, I was important, a person of value. In raising my son, He raised my self-worth and that of all those like me. In giving me back my son, He gave back my worth and dignity as a person. Would this ensure that death or trouble would never visit my house again? Certainly not! But it gave to me the knowledge that no matter what would happen in the days that followed, my life was worthwhile because I had met the Master. I am somebody, and that can never be taken from me.

"Oh Master and Redeemer, thank you for this act of love. As you restored her you have restored many to their rightful place in life… Amen."

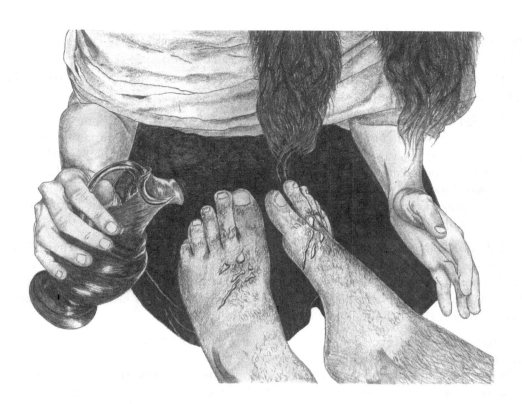

The Sinful Woman

Love for the Unloveables

Luke 7:36-50

Can you imagine what it would be like to be caught in a spider's web? Once caught, there is no escape. No amount of determination or will power will set you free. The more you struggle, the more entangled you become. Doomed… hopeless.

Some might say my journey into the spider's web was understandable, even excusable. My mother died bringing me into the world and my father cursed me for it. I lived with one relative after another, still a child, but on my own. And then there were men. When I turned twelve, they began to give me nice things, expecting things from me. At first, it was a traumatic experience being with men. But then I began to like the perfume, the silky clothing, the jewelry… the attention. I thought a few loved me, but they always left. I never had anyone love me. I didn't know what love was.

Why didn't I change? Give up that life? I didn't know how. I didn't know another way of life or even that there was another way. Besides, I was a captive and I could not have changed if I had wanted to. The demons were in complete possession of me.

"I want you to meet a man," a friend of mine said to me one day.

"Sure, sounds like fun," I quickly answered, still the harlot. "I didn't think there was a man left in Judea I hadn't met." Everyone laughed. Then I noticed my friend wasn't smiling. There was something strange about her. "Joanna, where are you taking me? Who is this man?"

She didn't say anything, only that she had arranged for me to meet Him. "There," she pointed, "there in the olive grove! Go!"

I untied my hair and pulled at my clothing. I walked up to Him and came on to Him like a harlot. When He turned, I saw His face and I drew back. It was the Galilean. I had heard of Him. He had saved a friend from stoning who was accused of adultery. He frightened me. He looked at me kindly and said to me that the world called me a harlot because of how I live to please men and because my pay is a harlot's pay. I turned away. Then He called me to come away from that life! He told me God's love is great and that His forgiveness is without limit. I just looked at Him. "What is love?" I asked.

I'll never forget His words about how the spider holds its prey tightly, and how God would free me. He would free me to be the child He created. "I have never been a child to anyone!" I sobbed. He was so gentle with me. He agreed that this was so, but He said that God had never deserted me, even during the worst of times. He said He had come to tell me that God loved me, His precious child.

His words were a revelation to me. No one had ever spoken to me with such love… such kindness… such understanding. As I gazed into His face with my tear-filled eyes, a warm feeling spread throughout my body. His words washed away my pain and filled me with a sense of hope. For the first time in my life, I believed that someone loved me for myself and cared enough for me to free me from this spider's web of self-hatred and personal destruction that had bound me fast for so many years. I knew that, if I believed, I could free myself of the demons that had me in their grasp.

That evening, I heard that Jesus was going to be at the home of Simon the Pharisee. I always carried with me my alabaster jar of perfume. I'd use it when men came to my room, or when I went to theirs. I crashed in on Simon's party with my jar of perfume. His servants grabbed me… after all, I was a sinful woman and had no right to trespass in the Pharisee's house… but Jesus motioned for them to leave me alone. Falling at Jesus' feet, I began once again to cry. But this time, they were tears of release and of joy! My tears fell on Jesus' dusty feet. I wiped His feet with my hair. As a denial of my former life and undying gratitude of the forgiveness I had been granted, I poured my entire jar of perfume on His feet.

I was no longer the sinful woman but a follower of Jesus… because I met the Master.

"Master, it is easy to get caught in the spider's web... keep me safe by keeping me close to you... Amen."

James, Jesus' Brother

Jesus' Concerned Family

Luke 8:19-21

He was the best big brother that any sister or brother could ask for… but He changed. We all noticed it. The change was subtle at first, but then it became quite obvious. Even our neighbors saw the change in Him.

Discreetly, they pulled Mother or me aside and asked about His well-being. When Father died, He took on that responsibility. To the younger sisters and brothers, He was the only father they knew. Our father died soon after my youngest sister was born. The change in our brother was very upsetting to them because they were afraid they'd lose another father figure.

Don't get me wrong He was still loving and gentle. I never saw Him get upset or become impatient with anyone. He always kept the Sabbath, but in His own way. Our Rabbi would get upset with Him when He'd help someone on the Sabbath, but Jesus always put people first. He was a role model for everyone in Nazareth. If anyone in the family or the village needed anything, He was right there to help in any way. You could always depend upon Jesus. My brothers and sisters adored Him. When He prayed before a meal, we felt we were hearing the voice of God. Everything was going so smoothly…why did He have to mess it up?

At first, it was the little things. He'd leave unfinished work on His work bench. He seemed to be preoccupied with something all the time. He was constantly going into the great wilderness alone to "commune with God" He'd say. One time He left with nothing to eat or drink and was gone for forty days and forty nights. When Mother told Him that we were all worried sick, He smiled and said what He had said since He was twelve years old, "Didn't you know I had to be in my Father's house?" *Luke 2:49*

For several weeks soon after that, He worked day and night fixing up our home and completing all the orders from His customers. Dressed for travel, He gave each of us a hug and talked alone with Mother, and then He left to begin His public ministry. He was thirty years old. Even something good can become too much. Religion is okay… no, it's good for a person. But too much can be a dangerous thing.

We heard disturbing stories of a Rabbi who was teaching with great authority, healing the sick, and standing up to the powers in Jerusalem. One day, we heard this Rabbi overturned the tables of the corrupted money changers in the Temple. "My house will be a house of prayer," we were told the Rabbi shouted, "but you have made it a den of robbers." *Luke 19:46* We knew it was Jesus. Large crowds were following Him. We even heard that He had raised a child from the dead.

Mother grew troubled; she asked us to find Him and bring Him home. We worried that He was beside Himself. None of us… except maybe for Mother… believed that He was divine, least of all me. He was my big brother. We wrestled as children... we played like normal children do. He was flesh and blood. He was no Messiah. Yet, that's what people were saying… that He was the Messiah, the Promised One. And while He could get away with people saying that up north in Galilee, Jerusalem was a different arena. We tried again and again to persuade Him not to go to Jerusalem for Passover that year. But He had set His mind on Jerusalem and no one could have stopped Him.

And there I found myself, standing at the foot of His cross. My big brother was dying before my eyes. Did I believe? I knew He did. But I was angry. Was this His Father's business to make Him die this hideous death? My big brother, whose only crime was to bring a message of love to a loveless world.

I'm not ashamed to say now that I still didn't believe, even when they found the empty tomb. After the Resurrection, Jesus appeared to many. Then He appeared to me alone. I was a hard sell; I took a lot of convincing. But I could not deny the truth of what was right in front of my eyes. My brother, whom I had seen die on the cross, stood in front of me. He embraced me—He forgave me my stubbornness. Then, He told me of God's plan for me.

He told me that His followers would remain in Jerusalem for a number of years. When the persecutions came, the fellowship of believers would be scattered to the ends of the earth. He said I would be the leader of the first church of Jerusalem.

"Yes, yes!" I proclaimed. I then believed. I had met the Master.

"Lord, grant me the greatness of heart to forgive rejection, to strive for understanding, to welcome change... in myself and in others... Amen."

Simon the Pharisee

Simon's Party

Luke 7:36-50

Yes, I met the Master. I want to go on record as saying, "I liked the man." I even had Him over for dinner. The trouble with Him was not what He did but how He did it. Take, for example, the night He came to my house for dinner.

The purpose of the dinner party was to give some of my fellow Pharisees the opportunity to get to know Jesus better. They simply did not like or trust Him. So, I stood up for Jesus, saying that if they'd just give Him a chance, they'd discover, as I had, that He wasn't all that bad. Unfortunately, it didn't turn out that way.

My friends left the party saying, "See, we told you so," and shouting that He had defiled my house by that spectacle with the prostitute. When I quietly made a comment about the inappropriateness of His actions, He launched into one of those famous stories of His. I have to confess I have a hard time understanding why others rave over them. I generally find these stories childish and difficult to understand. However, this story I understood. He likened me in the story to the debtor forgiven the least. He even made me answer the riddle of the story right in front of everyone. Then He turned to that woman and said that because she sinned much and repented much, her sins were forgiven much. Soon thereafter the party broke up in a big argument over who can or cannot forgive sins.

I've never given such a disastrous party in my life. My social status took a tumble because of the Master coming to my house for dinner. At first, I was angry… humiliated… I could not believe that He could be so ungrateful. But when I cooled down, I began to ponder on His words. He was teaching a radical new way of looking at things… at people. He insisted that every person had value, that every person was worthy of respect. He was telling us to let God judge people's actions and their worth. He was questioning our right and our ability to interpret the Law. It was a disturbing idea… and not one that was easy for me to swallow.

"Master, keep me from the blindness of the dinner host and from judging others unjustly. Help me see everyone as a child of God… Amen."

Mary Called Magdalene

Faithful to the End

Luke 8:1-2

The things you have heard about me are simply not true. First of all, I am not the woman who anointed Jesus at Simon's party, although many have confused us. I was there as a "respectable" follower of Jesus; however, I raised my hands to heaven and praised God when that beautiful woman gave her life to God, washed the Master's feet with her tears and her hair, and anointed Him with oil.

This is not to say that I didn't have a special role to play in Luke's story. I did, just as did Mary and Joseph and the many others mentioned in Luke's account. My special role was to care for Jesus, to take care of the details of His ministry so that He could concentrate on ushering in the Kingdom of God. Unlike most women who are not married or have no sons, I had a measure of wealth and I could afford to give my life to God and provide funds for Jesus' ministry. I was happy to do so. He restored my life; it was only right that I should dedicate the rest of my life to Him. I praise God for that day when we met for the first time near my home town of Magdala on the west shore of the Sea of Galilee. Our meeting place was also near Bethsaida where He fed the multitudes with only five loaves and two small fishes.

I went to see Him but was unable to due to the large crowd, so I began walking home. It was on my way home that we met. It was as if He planned for us to meet alone. We talked throughout the night. A quiet came over our conversation and then He asked me to believe in God, a God who is able to cast out the demons which plagued me both day and night for years. I was speechless. How did He know this? I was ashamed... then hopeful. He even knew how many demons possessed me. They were a curse. I had given up the battle with them. I began to cry. I cried until daybreak.

He told me to trust in God and my demons would be gone. I did and they were. I followed Him from that day forward. I was there at the cross... I was the first to see the empty tomb... I was the first to see the resurrected Master.

I often reflect on how I was healed and made well... it sometimes troubles me that I was healed while others were not. Most of those who are troubled or ill in Luke's stories don't receive healing, only a few do. Why was I one of the "few"? Jesus told us that He did not come into the world to heal our bodies but to give us strength to endure the hardships when they come with all their force. He had come to give us life... an abundant life... but more importantly, to bring us life eternal. Until He comes again, we must fight against the evil one, bring compassion into the world and love one another as He first loved us. We must give up living for ourselves so we can live for Him.

"Master, make me an instrument of your love. Help me to show those around me the promise of eternal life until you come again... Amen."

Legion

Possessed by Many Demons

Luke 8:26-39

Demon-possessed... swine crashing into the sea... a naked, crazy man living among the dead, never living in a house like a normal person... devils... a legion of them pleading with the son of God not to be cast into the abyss.

Can you believe such a story? I am told that it happened… to me! Fuzzy memories, a bad dream. They told me that I was possessed by a legion of devils. It was I who lived among the tombs. I was the battle ground where the Son of the Most High fought with and vanquished the legions from Hell. How amazing!

But what was much more astonishing to me was that many of the townspeople held me responsible for the loss of their pigs. For them, the sight of their herds floating belly-up in the lake was a greater tragedy than the sight of me as a raging, uncontrollable madman. What Jesus did came at a price… His decision to cast the demons out of me and into the pigs caused them to charge into the lake and drown. I'm afraid if presented with the option the people would have said, "Let him stay the way he is!" Jesus gave me back my life, my sanity, my soul. But for the townsfolk, the price was too steep.

I know the loss of their pigs would have had a financial impact on their families. However, they were able to retrieve most of the hogs from the lake and butcher them, so it wasn't a total loss. Yet, it's difficult to believe that people could think that way. To them, it was better that I suffer than their pigs drown! I often wonder who was actually possessed… me, by the legions of demons, or them, by their own possessions? It was the old story; they had placed their trust in things and look how easily those things were taken from them.

But that is all in the past. I worked hard and paid them for what loss they had incurred. I seldom see those people any more. I travel to as many places as possible, telling one and all about what I was then and who I am now. All because I met the Master.

"Master, help me put the welfare of people first, my purse last, and to place my future in you… Amen."

Jairus

She is Not Dead

Luke 8:40-42, 49-56

I wanted to shout from the rooftop, "The Lord be praised! He raised my daughter from the dead!" But I was to tell no one and so I obeyed. However, the good physician has now told you, so I don't think the Master would mind if I break my silence.

It was not the first time I had met the Master, I am ashamed to say. I had met Him previously at the door to my synagogue. Do you hear that? *My* synagogue. How arrogant!

As leader of the synagogue, it was my responsibility to be sure every aspect of the Law was strictly obeyed. Word reached me about the Galilean. Some said He was a miracle worker, the long awaited Messiah. Other leaders said He was a troublemaker who misinterpreted the Torah to further his own ambition. In some Sabbath gatherings, He had almost started riots. His own synagogue in Nazareth… why… they tried to throw Him off a cliff. I vowed that He'd cause no trouble in my synagogue!

The day finally came. I called the council members together and told them that I planned to block the entrance to the synagogue if He should try to enter. Some protested, saying this was God's house, and no one should be kept from entering. In the end, I had my way (I always did!). He came and I was ready. I met Him face-to-face and told Him that He wasn't welcome. He looked around and said that perhaps we didn't need a physician and walked on. I was irate! He won… I lost! I despised Him and said so during worship.

"Beware of false prophets," I preached. Oh God, how blind and stupid I was!

A few months later my only daughter became ill. She was just twelve years old. Each day her condition worsened. I thought surely God would not take my daughter, the daughter of his most respected Rabbi. But it seemed like He might. I could do nothing. I was powerless. Holding her in my arms, I could feel her life slowly drain from her body. One morning, she did not open her eyes. I placed my ear to her chest. Thank God, she was still breathing, but faintly... oh, so faintly. I clutched her to my chest as I begged God to spare her. But my family and friends had already begun to mourn her. "Stop!" I shouted. "She is not dead."

"There is no hope," they responded. "The physicians cannot help her. It is just a matter of time."

"NO!" I cried as I ran from the house. "NO! NO! NO!" I knew that I was out of earthly options. My one hope... my only hope... was Him.

I ran and ran and finally came upon a large crowd. There in the middle was the Galilean. I had no pride left. I stopped before Him and fell to my knees. I pleaded with Him to do what He would with me, to punish me in any way He saw fit for my arrogance, but please, please could He save my innocent daughter? As I lay groveling there before Him, one of my servants came from my house to tell me my daughter was dead. He reached down and helped me to my feet. He told me to have faith, to believe, and my daughter would be healed. After stopping to heal one last person in the crowd... a woman with some kind of bleeding ailment... He went to my daughter's side... and you know the rest. He took my dead daughter by the hand and told her to get up and she stood up. As I fell to my knees in gratitude, He turned to me and said to me that God had allowed my daughter to sleep so that I could awaken. That she appeared to be dead but was not, just as I appeared to be alive but was not.

"Forgive me, Lord," I begged Him. "I have placed things before people. I have sinned. Forgive me."

He told me I was forgiven as the words left my mouth. He told me to rise and be God's man and to never close the doors leading to God's Kingdom... and I never have.

"Master, it's easy to become so puffed up with the feeling of self-importance. Help me to keep from doing this. I pray for healing in my family... Amen."

The Woman Bleeding

Who Touched Me?

Luke 8:43-48

What in the world have I done? I thought to myself the moment I did it. *Oh God, forgive me. I have defiled the Rabbi.* For twelve years I have been suffering. My issue of blood, something which no doctor was able to cure, made me a social outcast. I was free to come and go as long as I touched no one and no one touched me. Do you know what it's like to live twelve years without feeling the touch of another? The hemorrhaging, the fatigue, the isolation… this and more I could have dealt with. What hurt me most was not being able to hug my grandchildren or touch my children and their father. If I just brushed against them, they had to ritually bathe in order to be cleansed.

And there He was, passing right in front of me… the Rabbi from Galilee, the Healer… the one who touched lepers and made them clean. Surely I could touch Him. But would I have the strength? I had forgotten how to reach out. I was so conditioned not to touch, that when my chance to be cured was before me, I was afraid to. *Oh God, I just can't… I just can't.* But I did!

I fell to my knees. What had I done? *Please … please, oh God, let no one notice.* Above the noise of the crowd I heard the Galilean ask, "Who touched me?" *Luke 8:45*

Oh no, I thought, *this man of God has felt the unclean touch of this sinner.* His disciples implied that the group was so large that many were touching Him. Jesus would not budge. He had felt keenly that one touch. I staggered to my feet and fell before Him, begging His forgiveness. When I tried to press my case, the crowd, hearing that I was unclean, fell back. Then a strange feeling came over me. A… a… power washed over me and… praise God… could it be? Yes, it was… I was cured. "I am cured! Praise God Almighty, I am cured!" I cried.

What did He mean when He said my faith had cured me? I pondered this as I walked home. People kept coming up to me, hugging me, touching me and telling me how happy they were for me. I smiled. How good another's touch felt. How good it was to be clean. But how did my faith cure me? My "faith." Was that it? I hadn't known I had faith or that I had used it. I simply turned to God. I reached out to Him, not knowing the outcome. I had risked humiliation, chastisement and even ridicule for the one remote possibility that I'd be touched by God. That was it! It must have been. That moment, that fleeting moment, when I turned it all over to God. Look what that one moment of faith did for me. What are the possibilities of a lifetime of faith?

I met the Master. I touched Him once. He touched me greatly.

Later, I discovered that Jairus' daughter was twelve years old when Jesus healed her. I had suffered from bleeding for twelve years when Jesus healed me. The year I first prayed to God for healing, twelve years ago, Jairus' daughter was born. Sometimes, a prayer can take a while to be answered.

"Master, such little faith can do so much. May my faith grow each day... Amen."

The Worried Father

Not Another Night

Luke 9:37-43

Night after night I sat beside his bed. Praying and wondering, *What would tomorrow bring? Would my prayers be heard at last? Would they be answered? Or would it be another day of living hell?* When I'd look at my son, I had to fight with myself… to keep from asking the Lord to take him in his sleep. At night he was still and peaceful. In the morning the demons would have their play with him… sudden screams, a twisted face… foaming of the mouth. *Oh Lord, I cannot face another day of this,* I thought.

I heard that a few of the disciples of the Galilean were close by. I took my boy to them. I asked them to lay their hands on him and set him free of those demons that possessed him. They did as I requested. I knew my son would be cured. The Rabbi had taught them well. They prayed with power, authority and compassion. When they finished my son was calm, but he then fell into convulsions more violently than ever before. After I had restrained him and the seizures were lessening, I looked up at the disciples. They were noticeably upset. They had failed. They felt powerless. To justify themselves, they implied that my boy's condition was due to the sins of his parents. *My fault!* After they collected themselves, they expressed sorrow for what they had said. Then they left.

As the days passed and my son's condition did not change, I decided to take him to the source of healing, the Master Himself. I searched and searched and finally found Him.

The crowd was all around… I couldn't get through. I shouted and finally I was heard. The disciples had told Jesus about me and He expressed disappointment for the way they had responded to my situation. Just then my son, weary from the journey, succumbed to the demons. Jesus pushed me aside and... well, the physician tells it correctly... I cannot begin to describe for you how this worried father felt, seeing his son stand upright, slightly smiling, the demons gone.

What did I learn from all of this? Many things, but one in particular. There is no substitute for meeting the Master… for going to Him directly… always in prayer and sometimes through others. Things can only be taken care of by bringing them to Him. I thank God I took my boy to the Master and that we, my son and I, met Him that day.

"Master, the nights can be long and the days never ending when a loved one is ill... bring healing to my home... Amen."

The Would-Be Disciple

The Cost is High

Luke 9:57-62

There were many of us who would have followed Him, you know! People often wonder why there were so few disciples. Well, the reason is… let's face it… He discouraged people. That's right! He not only discouraged us, He downright made it difficult... no... impossible! Not that I'm trying to make a case for myself, like the others. But they would say the same. It's true. He confused us. On the one hand He would say the harvest was plentiful and that there was need for many more workers. And then when we stepped up, He discouraged us.

Take the day I first met the Master. Oh, I had heard Him speak on many occasions. I often talked with His disciples. After much consideration, I made my decision to follow Him. Luke mentions two others who expressed a desire to follow Him that day. Actually, they were two of many. But when they heard Jesus' demands, they just walked away, shaking their heads. He was simply asking too much, too abruptly. People shouldn't be asked to make such radical sacrifices on the spur of the moment. Over time, perhaps, but not on the spot like that. Besides, where's the harm in a man wanting to bury his father, or another wanting to say goodbye to family and friends before going off to follow Jesus? Those are good and noble desires. Why did He make them part of His conditions? As for me... well, I had taken care of all those loose ends. So, I stepped up and said, "I'm ready!" I was sure I was prepared to make the commitment.

But the Master picked up on my uncertainty. He knew that my dedication wasn't absolute. I had questions. What did the future have in store for me if I followed Him? One of the would-be disciples was turned away by the Master because he kept looking back. I kept trying to only look ahead but I was troubled by what I could not see. So, I left with the others and walked home.

Sometime later, word reached me that the Master had been crucified. I was saddened but not surprised. He had been headed for just such a harsh ending. He demanded too much. The strict demands He placed upon His life and the lives of those who wanted to follow Him alienated them and added fuel to the fire the Pharisees were preparing for Him. I will say, I can now understand why He required such a commitment from His followers. To follow Him all the way to the cross required more commitment than I had.

Yes, I met the Master. I wanted to be His disciple. Now I don't know whether that would have been a good idea.

"Oh, Master, to be so close... help me make the commitment to follow you and then rely upon your strength to fulfill it... Amen."

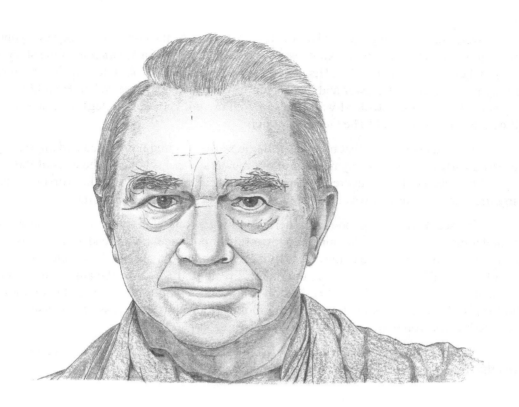

The Scholar

Neighbor

Luke 10:25-37

I tried to put Jesus to the test by asking Him a question in front of a large group of people. I thought he'd answer the question with a lengthy, philosophical answer, which would lose everyone and disclose Jesus as nothing but a fraud. Instead, He caught me off guard with a swift comeback to my question of "What must I do to inherit eternal life?" *Luke 10:25* He asked a two part question, "What is written in the Law?" and "How do you read it?" *Luke 10:26*

All eyes were on me then. I answered Him with the first thing that came to my mind. Something I had learned when I was a small boy. Something every Israelite knows and prays morning, noon and night… the most important prayer in the Jewish prayer book… the "Shema." "Hear, O Israel, the Lord our God, the Lord is One… You shall love the Lord your God with all your heart, soul, strength, and mind." *Deuteronomy 6:4-5* Also, you shall love your neighbor as yourself." *Leviticus 19:18*

He said I had answered correctly. "Do this and you shall live!" He said. *Luke 10:28*

Wait a minute! I thought. *Who's asking the questions? Who's being put to the test, here?* With the speed of an angry asp, I fired back, "Well, who is my neighbor?" I knew I had Him then. He had no way out, because to Jesus everyone was a neighbor. If He started with a "we are all brothers" speech, folks in this crowd wouldn't buy it.

Well, the next thing I knew He was telling a story. At the end of His story everyone, including me, was taken with the kindness of, well, of all people, a *Samaritan* in the story. We were so taken that when He asked His next question, I fell for it hook, line and sinker. I gave the only possible correct answer and once again, I was put in my place. When He told me to "go and do likewise," *Luke 10:37* I walked away with my tail between my legs. People began calling the story Jesus told "The Good Samaritan."

I walked away from that meeting with the Master feeling humiliated and angry. My ego was greatly damaged, to say nothing of my reputation as a scholar in the eyes of the people. I had been out-maneuvered by an uneducated carpenter. That was the worst moment in my life. Yet, I see now it was the best thing that could have happened to me.

You see, I was flying too high. There's nothing wrong with flying, except that what was under my wings was the hot air of my own self-importance. I was headed for a crash. Sooner or later it would have come. I was flying so high I could not see those below me. Even with all of my education, status, and importance, I really did not know the answer to the most important question of life. If you do not know who your neighbor is, then you do not know who God is. Without that knowledge you are fooling yourself. Regardless of expensive robes and large houses, you don't know who you really are.

Yes, I met the Master. He popped my bubble. I landed right next to my neighbor. From that time on, I've decided to walk instead of fly.

"Master, show me my neighbor and give me the courage to reach out and help when my neighbor is in need... Amen."

Martha

No Time to Smell the Roses

Luke 10:38-42

      Hi, I'm Martha. I am the compulsive, workaholic type. Compulsive… never sitting down… always doing something. Then there's my younger sister Mary… she enjoys life, every minute of it. She stops to smell the roses while I am clearing the tables! We make a good pair. I work, she takes walks! I rake leaves, she plays in them. I weed the garden, she picks flowers in the meadow. And I suppose you might say I am also a complainer. Well, you'd complain, too. I do all the work and Mary has all of the fun.

      Well, there we were. Our dear friend, Jesus, the most important person in all of Judea and Galilee was coming to our house for dinner and, wouldn't you know it, Mary hadn't lifted her hand to help me one time. I was stuck making all of the meal preparations and she was the life of the party, the perfect hostess. Well, I had had enough and I told her so right there in front of the Rabbi. He is a hard-working teacher, always on the go, so, I had thought for sure that He'd side with me and get Mary hopping. But what do you think happened? Luke has it right. He sided with Mary! I was flabbergasted!

      Who prepared the food, served the meal, made Him comfortable? Me, that's who! So, I had thought I'd get a little sympathy and Mary would get a little lecture on taking her responsibilities more seriously! But, oh no, He didn't support me, right there in front of everyone! Fuming, I went to the kitchen, His words still ringing in my head.

As I looked out the window, I thought about what He said. The Rabbi didn't use words carelessly. All of His words had a deeper meaning... a personalized message to all around Him. I knew He was trying to tell me something, but what was it? He had sided with Mary, but why? He didn't say that I should act like Mary, He didn't criticize what I was doing. He had thanked me often during the evening. No, that wasn't it!

He was critical of my motives. My motives were self-serving; I had tried to impress others and make Mary look bad. Why did I complain to the Master? So that he'd praise me and scold Mary!

He told me that life was more than what we do. Life is being... being in fellowship with God, and pleasing Him. You are known to God not for what you do, but for who you are. Yes, I met the Master and He changed my life. It's never too late to change. Oh, I still need to keep busy, but now I enjoy life more and appreciate every day. If it was possible for me, it is for you, too.

"Cleanse my heart, Master. Make my motives pure. May my work be done without shouts of praise... Amen."

Woman in the Crowd

Hurt Feelings

Luke 11:27-28

What did I say that was so wrong? Why did the Rabbi come down on me so hard, right there in front of everyone? I was waiting a long time for that moment. I had thought about what I'd say. I had rehearsed it over and over. I wanted it to be just right, to bring glory to this man I had watched from afar and admired so. And then to be cut down… in front of my friends!

I had thought those words would bring great honor to the Galilean's mother. Didn't He honor His mother? Of course He did! So, why did He throw my words back into my face? At the time, I did not want to think any further. He had hurt my feelings and I was angry. To have my words turn His thoughts and words to this "wicked generation." Well, I left and went home. It was too much.

As hard as I tried, I could not get what happened out of my mind. Especially His words, "Blessed rather are those who hear the word of God and obey it." Luke 11:28 I suppose I could have said that, but I thought He'd like a word of praise for Himself... His mother. No, He didn't want praise. To my embarrassment, He made that perfectly clear.

More than anything else He wanted people to hear and keep God's word. The Rabbi did not want to win a popularity contest. It wasn't important that people liked Him... or approved of His actions. He didn't deliberately try to hurt people by what He said or did, but

He came into the world to save it; nothing was more important than that. The way the world would be saved was by His people hearing and keeping God's word. He would, if necessary, embarrass, challenge, confront, and do all He could to get His message across.

I am glad I met the Master and that He was more concerned with my soul than my pride. Despite my hurt feelings, I knew He loved me. I finally realized that nothing would deter Him… neither criticism nor praise… from His purpose in the world.

"Show me how, Lord, to give you not only praise but to hear and keep your word in my life... Amen."

The Squeaky Clean Pharisee

Wash Up

Luke 11:37-54

All I said was, "Wash up!"

If I had thought He would react the way He did, I would have kept my mouth shut. Now really, was "Wash up before you eat" too much to ask? Why was He so troubled? Everything He said seemed a little uncalled for, don't you think? He became so upset. He challenged every Pharisee there, and you know the Pharisees are the strict keepers of the Law of Moses. His accusations ended the party (to put it mildly). In reality He almost started a riot. I thought this would be an occasion for the others to get to understand Jesus better, to realize He wasn't all that bad. Was I ever mistaken! He went on and on about the Pharisees and the Law. When my scholar friend tried to point out that His words were insulting, He challenged the scholars. By the time He finished, all of them were going after Him. He didn't make any friends that night. Instead, He made plenty of enemies.

But again, I have to ask you, what's so terrible about washing before you eat? Of course, I realize that this means something totally different in your time than it did in ours. To you washing is for sanitary reasons. We knew little of those considerations. To us, it had to do with keeping clean according to the Law. Even if our hands were squeaky clean we'd still wash before eating.

That was the Law. So was tithing, and He attacked that too, accusing us of keeping only the letter of the Law, down to enforcing a tithe "mint, rue and all other kinds of garden herbs." *Luke 11:42* The Rabbi spoke correctly, as well He should. He was raised by Hebrew parents. He knew the Law. Wasn't He a Rabbi? Why couldn't He just stick to the Law and stop creating a commotion over something as unimportant as, yes, a mint leaf! What was the big deal? Who was He to accuse us of neglecting justice and the love of God? His words cut to the quick. He said we were squeaky clean on the outside, but dirty on the inside.

Hypocrites! Greedy! Wicked! That's what He had called us. But, it wasn't us. We were just doing what God commanded us to do. So be it. It was our responsibility and obligation to obey the Law and make sure others did the same.

Do you understand what was so wrong with my simple request, "Wash before you eat?" Yes, I met the Master and I still don't know what really happened at my party.

"To be smug... to look down my nose at others because life has not blessed them with the things needed to be worldly clean. Keep me from this, oh Master... Amen."

The Woman Bent Over

Set Free

Luke 13:10-17

To be perfectly honest, I was watching an ant crawl across the floor of the synagogue. Yes, an ant. It was trying to carry something many times its own size. It would not give up. It pushed and pulled. It stopped, rested and considered its next move. It never gave up. At times the weight of the object seemed to be too much for it to carry.

How disrespectful, you might think. Watching an ant instead of listening to the Rabbi. Well, don't you ever daydream? You may look out the window… I look down at the floor. I can do no other. For you see, I had been bent over for eighteen years, unable to look another in the face as we pass, or even to look up to see if it were going to rain. For eighteen years, I had the pity of the community. They meant well. I'd accepted it. I was determined to make the best of my life, even if the president of the synagogue tried to make me feel like it was my own fault. He was probably embarrassed that his prayers for my healing hadn't helped at all.

"He's talking to you," I heard someone say, pulling my attention from the ant.

"Who?" I asked, as I turned my head. "The young Rabbi."

"Get up, woman," they said, "He wants you to come to Him."

"No," I said, not wanting to be an object lesson for the morning message, nor did I want to have some itinerate preacher practice his healing on me. I had had enough of those characters.

"He's different," they urged. "This is Jesus of Nazareth."

"Oh," I said. I had heard of Him. They said He was like no other. I agreed to walk to the front. The leader of the synagogue saw what was happening. He stepped between us to stop me. The Master reached out and pulled me past the priest. Then the Rabbi spoke. I'll never forget His words. He gestured toward my poor crippled back and said that Satan meant this affliction for evil, but that God meant it for good.

"Woman, you are set free from your infirmity." *Luke 13:12* He laid His hand on my back. A tingling sensation traveled up my spine. My muscles contracted, pulling me straight up. Something popped in my back and I was able to stand up straight. Oh, did that feel good! I slowly bent down and up again... and again… and again! I was healed! I was healed! I began praising God and the others joined me. The priest criticized Jesus harshly for healing me on the Sabbath but the Master put him in his place. All the rest of the congregation shared my joy in my healing.

I often think of that day, the day I was healed. The day I met the Master. If I had stayed at home I never would have met Him or been healed. God will do His part. We must do ours. I thank God that I did not stay home that day and pity myself. Getting up and going to worship made it possible for me to meet the Master and for Him to heal me.

"Straighten us up, Master, so we can walk erect and be a witness to your love and healing... Amen."

The Ruling Pharisee

Not on the Sabbath

Luke 14:1-24

It is a great responsibility being the person in charge. Much is expected of you... not only by the people and your peers... but also by God. As a Pharisee who was part of our ruling council, the Sanhedrin, I was placed in such a position. I always had to be on the lookout for those who would fall upon my people like wolves upon sheep. By whatever means necessary, I had to make sure that false prophets were quickly discovered and exposed. This was the reason for inviting the Galilean to my house after synagogue that Sabbath. I planned to expose Him as someone who did not follow the Law. How could He be a prophet if He did not follow our Laws?

Our plan was to sit Him beside a member of my congregation who had dropsy. We heard the Galilean was healing people on the Sabbath, which violates the Law of Moses. We even heard that a woman was healed right in the synagogue. Think of it... and on the Sabbath too! This man would be our bait. "Oh, don't worry about him," I reassured the other priests. "He's so ill he can hardly keep his eyes open. He'll sleep right through it."

Everyone was in place, and as expected, my friend fell asleep face down (literally) in his dish of food. What a sight! The Galilean saw him and then questioned us about healing on the Sabbath. He was a clever one; He had caught on to what we were trying to do. Yet, He went ahead and healed the man anyway and sent him home. We were prepared to accuse Him of breaking the Law when He asked questions we could not answer. He twisted the Law and its interpretation so that we could not retaliate.

He then criticized us for sitting at the places of honor. He told me I should have invited the poor, the crippled. Why? So that I would be rewarded in heaven. One of my Pharisee friends tried to lighten things up by saying something nice, "Blessed is the one who will eat at the feast in the kingdom of God" or something like that. *Luke 14:15* But the Rabbi rebuked him with one of His stories, which was critical of our only inviting reputable people to our gatherings.

I'm sure I can speak for my friends when I say I was glad when that dinner ended. What a miserable fiasco. Okay, maybe He wasn't invited for the proper reason. Maybe we were trying to catch Him defiling the Sabbath by changing this man's condition. But that's our job. We were trying to uphold the Law, and then He brings up all that business of poverty, the lost and those seeking salvation. What was the point of all that?

Yes, I met the Master. I hope I don't have to meet Him again.

"Dine this day at my house, Master, and may I never put you to a test... Amen."

Man with Dropsy

The Trap

Luke 14:1-4

Oh, how my feet and hands ached! They were all swollen, and my stomach was bloated like a pig. My only relief was to sleep, which I did more and more often.

One day I was invited to a Sabbath meal being held at the home of a prominent Pharisee. Little did I know then that the reason I was invited was to bait a trap set for another guest. Those Pharisees were really opposed to Jesus healing on the Sabbath. They called it a defilement of the Law. They placed me next to the guest of honor, Jesus. I thought this seating arrangement was a bit odd. Well, I discovered later, they knew that in time I'd be unable to keep my eyes open and they wanted me to be in plain view of Jesus.

The next thing I knew I heard someone calling my name. I thought it was a dream. I woke up. I felt strange. Always before, when I woke up I felt groggy and listless, and it took some time for me to become completely alert. This time, however, I was wide awake, alert and refreshed. I discovered that I had awakened in the middle of a heated argument between Jesus and my Pharisee friends. Jesus walked me to the door and told me to be on my way. Another dinner guest caught up with me and told me what was going on. He told me that the Galilean had healed me!

I could not believe him. I sat down outside of town underneath a sycamore tree. I stayed there until dusk. I cried with joy. The swelling and pain were gone. The man was telling the truth. I was healed! Praise the Lord! Coming up the road, only a few paces away, was a group of people, about twelve to fourteen of them. One was the Master. I slowly walked over to Him. I got down on my knees and thanked Him for what he had done for me. My friend had used me, but Jesus showed me compassion. My friend often made fun of me. The Master saw nothing humorous in my situation. No one had ever taken me or my illness seriously until that night when the Master did. They used me, but Jesus cared about me. Because of them, I met the Master and He made me whole.

"Master, help me endure the pains of life and find my relief in you... Amen."

The Thankful Leper

The Samaritan?

Luke 17:11-19

Being brought back to life from a living hell... from a fate worse than death! That is how I'd describe being cured of leprosy.

There were ten of us. Before we became lepers, we never would have been seen together, much less lived together, as we did as lepers. The others never would have spoken to me, nor would I have spoken to them. They were Jews, and I, a Samaritan. There had been a feud between our people going back hundreds of years. While I'm not sure exactly what started the feud, I knew that intermarriage… a lack of racial purity… was at the root of it. Our people had become bitter enemies.

Whatever happened to cause such animosity between our races was of little concern. We had a greater common enemy to fight… Leprosy. It had reduced us all to the same level. A leper was a leper… the same rules applied. It made no difference whether you were a Jew, a Samaritan, a woman or a man, you were only a leper.

The day we met the Master, the others rushed up to Him, pleading with Him to have pity on us. I stayed back. He was a Jew. I was not one of His kind. If He could heal us, as we had heard, I assumed His hatred for Samaritans in general would be stronger than His pity for one lowly Samaritan leper.

He simply told us to go and show ourselves to the priests. On nothing more than faith they turned, grabbed hold of me and pulled me along with them. I looked back. The Master just stood there quietly, looking at us. About a mile down the road we looked at our arms, then at one another's faces. We could not believe it. We were healed! Oh God, could it be? Had we really been rescued from this hell?

We started running as fast as we could. Suddenly I stopped. The others continued running to the Temple, not noticing or caring that I was not with them. "Stop… stop!" I shouted. "We should not be going that way! We should be going back to the Master." The others just kept running. "He's the one. He's the one." I continued to yell. They soon were out of sight.

I went back and fell before Him, praising and thanking God. Why did I go back? Because He cured me! Yes! But more… I was a Samaritan! He healed a Samaritan leper! He reached over the barrier of prejudice and hatred and treated me like a human being. It made no difference who I was, only that I was in need.

"May I always thank you, Master, for your goodness… my first words of the morning and last at night… Amen."

The Rich Ruler

Give All to the Poor

Luke 18:18-30

I was rich and a ruler of my people. That's how the physician saw me. I suppose he was correct. But please understand that wealth is relative! To my people I was very wealthy. To the Romans I was just an average citizen. I won't quibble over it; I had more than most. But for me, all this wealth was of no interest. Rich or poor… what matters most is the soul. Whether you are a beggar or a rich man like me, eternal life should occupy our minds every waking moment.

I used to be concerned because there were so many around me with so little and I had so much. Then I reasoned, *It isn't this life that is important but the next. So, there are people who are suffering. It won't last. So, I live in splendor. That too, won't last! What the poor need is the courage to turn their attention to the glory of the life to come instead of dwelling on the misery of the life that is.*

This way of thinking was what brought me to meet the Master on that day. People said He spoke with authority and possessed wisdom beyond any man. I had not come to trick Him like the others had. I was sincere and honest. When I met Him, I called Him "good" out of respect. I was taken aback when He threw my compliment back into my face and then treated me like a school boy. He lectured me about the Ten Commandments. Of course, I knew the Commandments. I had kept the commandments ever since I learned them as a small child. I knew that I was a good and righteous person… I just wanted to be sure I was doing everything I could religiously to ensure my place in heaven. But when I asked Him about eternal life, about heaven and the world to come... what did He do? He pointed to the people all around Him and said that I should give to the poor all that I have! I was dumbfounded. I had been given my wealth by God and that was my place in this world… just as the poor had been given their place. I was seeking eternal life and He wanted me to climb down into the dirt and squalor of this world.

I was embarrassed and everyone could see it. Was it because I was very rich? No, I had nothing to be embarrassed about! My wealth was part of my God-given inheritance. I was embarrassed because He was challenging my sincerity and my understanding of the purpose of life… this life… the life lived not for the future but here and now, in this world. To Him, it was a matter of concern that people suffered and He saw this as a reason to try and change the natural order of things! Incredible! I had thought that since life was so temporary, changing earthly situations didn't matter. But to the Master it did! I was confused. I had thought knowledge and compliance would get me to heaven, not actions.

His words made me sad. Why should I have to give up what was mine by right and work to change the circumstances of others who were also living in the manner God had decreed for them? Surely that would distract me from ensuring that I was as worthy as possible? The Master had been watching me closely to see my reaction to His words. I could tell He was disappointed. He turned His back on me and spoke to His disciples, "How hard it is for the rich to enter the kingdom of God! Indeed, it is easier for a camel to go through the eye of a needle than for someone who is rich to enter the kingdom of God." *Luke 18:24-25*

This caused a lot of murmuring amongst the crowd. You see, while not many people were as rich as I was, they usually clung to their small comforts and valued themselves by comparison with those who had less than they did. Someone was brave enough to speak up and ask, "Who, then, can be saved?" *Luke 18:26*

The Master replied, "What is impossible with man is possible with God." *Luke 18:27* One of His disciples pointed out that His most constant companions had indeed left everything to follow Him. That may have been true, but really, how much did they have to start with? A small boat? Some nets? And what had they been promised as a reward?

"Truly I tell you," Jesus said to the crowd, "no one who has left home or wife or brothers or sisters or parents or children for the sake of the kingdom of God will fail to receive many times as much in this age, and in the age to come eternal life." *Luke 18:29-30*

Well! I really had to think about this. I wasn't ready yet to give up everything for this Master, but He had some really radical ideas that I wanted to think about… ideas that I'd never considered before. Maybe I'd come back and listen to Him again while He was in town and see if I could talk to Him some more… see if He could convince me…

"May nothing possess me except you, oh, Lord and Master... Amen."

The Blind Man

From Blindness to Tentmaking

Luke 18:35-43

By now you have begun to notice that the beloved physician, Luke, has told his story through the eyes of many who were crippled, diseased, and possessed. It is only natural that these healing events made a special impression upon Luke, the Good Physician. For him, they were more than curiosities... they were of great medical interest. More than anyone, he knew of their incredible nature. He knew there was no trickery, no hoax. The Master's touch had caused healing as no other touch could. I'm sure the physician was skeptical at first. No doubt he made many inquiries and did many examinations before he reached his conclusions. That is what brought him to me.

As with the others before me, I too was healed by the Master. I often walk by that very spot near Jericho thinking of the years I sat there begging for alms. The day I met the Master changed my life. He not only gave me back my sight, He restored my manhood. I was no longer a beggar at the mercy of others. I was now again the tentmaker. That was my profession before I was struck blind.

I remember how, on that day, the crowd tried to keep me quiet. I was an embarrassment to them. They didn't want the Master to think their fair city was filled with impertinent, homeless beggars. But praise God, Jesus pushed them and their insensitive snobbery aside and came to me, the blind beggar. He didn't go to the leading dignitaries who had gathered to welcome Him to Jericho, but came to me.

Luke wanted to know the entire story, just as I'm telling it to you years later. Luke examined my eyes, asked me many questions, and spoke to people who had known me all my life. He wrote it all down. As he was preparing to leave, I asked him if I'd ever go blind again. He asked me what type of blindness I meant. We smiled. We knew that for those who have met the Master and received Him into their hearts, there is no blindness, no darkness ever again. God healed my eyes. But more importantly, He gave me eternal sight.

"Give me, Oh God, the sight needed to see the things that are invisible to this world... the things of eternal worth and importance... Amen."

Zacchaeus

Up a Tree

Luke 19:1-10

     I see that you have met Levi the tax collector. Well, meet his boss. That's me! I am Zacchaeus, superintendent of taxes (very rich and, may I add, much despised). My riches, they said, came to me at the expense of the people. The Romans, or me… I don't know who they hated most. I guess you might say that I was the wealthiest, most disliked man in all of Jericho. I loved it. With lots of money, I could have anything; their hatred, well, that told me they noticed me. All of my life I had been ignored. Made fun of… "puny, little Zacchaeus," they used to say. Well, no one laughed any longer. They weren't applauding, but I had never had any hope that they'd ever do that. They got exactly what they deserved for the way they treated me.

     At first all of the wealth, hatred, and revenge gave me a strange comfort, but it faded. Yes, I had become the wealthiest, but also the loneliest man in all of Jericho. Getting even with people has a short payoff period. I had it all, but I still was not happy. I didn't have anyone with whom to share it. If I'd lost all my riches, my few friends would have been gone in a second. I thought wealth was the way to become a big man. But I was still the same size, except I had actually become smaller… inside, where it counts.

     Listen, I was more surprised than anyone when the Master looked up at me and made His announcement. At first I thought He had made a mistake. But I was the only one up in the tree, so it wasn't a mistake. He even called me by name. The others tried to dissuade Him but He would have it no other way. I tell you, walking home alongside the most important man in all Galilee and Judea, I felt ten feet tall. Because He was important? No, because He called me by name and chose my house to dine.

Before, no one had ever given me that kind of attention. No one had ever been that kind to me. As children, the others played tricks on me and later they tried to steal my money. But no one had ever treated me as the Master did. He didn't want anything in return… only me, only my friendship. I had climbed up in the tree to peek at the celebrity. But He went out on a limb to show me friendship… me, a hated tax collector.

Well, Luke has told you the rest. What I did next sounds generous to some, crazy to others. You don't know how generous, how crazy! Giving away half my wealth and riches? You see, without my position and riches I was once again just "puny little Zacchaeus." But that was okay. I had met the Master and I knew how tall I stood in the sight of God.

"The world might despise and hate me but you, Master, honor and love me with your presence. May I show my appreciation by reaching out to another this day… Amen."

Man with the Colt

Returned Blessed

Luke 19:28-40

Everybody wants to feel special in some way. To have something that sets you apart from the rest… not to brag about but to give you that feeling. A feeling, deep inside that says, especially during those shaky times, that you're okay. You are special.

To some, it's their family. "My family is famous and wealthy," they might say. To others, it might be their strength, as it was for Samson. Or maybe it's their intelligence, their wisdom, as it was for Solomon. It may even be something small… like... being the gatekeeper at the Temple. It makes no difference what it is… just something that makes you feel special. Do you know what I mean? Well, what made me feel special was my colt.

That's right, my colt. True, others had such an animal. Some had many animals. But my colt was special. It had never been ridden. Many people passed through my village on their way to Jerusalem, pilgrims going into the holy city, especially at Passover time. Oh, how they'd all stop and admire my colt. It was special and that made me feel special, too. That's what I mean… just that feeling inside, deep inside. You know! Then one day all of that was taken from me.

I had met the Master several times before. I suppose you could say I was His follower. Well, not quite. I hadn't made up my mind. I truly believed Him to be sent from God, unlike other men. I had seen the things He did. I had heard the words He spoke. No man could have done those things or spoken with such authority unless He was from God.

Yet something stood in the way of my giving myself completely to Him. The Master saw my hesitation and discouraged me from becoming a disciple until I resolved my internal conflict. Total commitment, that's what He required... nothing less.

Then His disciples said the Master had need of my colt. I can't tell you the feeling I had as I watched His disciples take that colt from me. I saw what made me special being led away. I felt empty inside. Then suddenly I understood. All the Master's actions had one goal... to lead men and women to God. He showed me what was standing between me and following Him. All things, like my colt, can be taken away. But I am special because I am a child of God. I am special for no other reason than because God loves me. The knowledge that I am His can never be taken away.

The Master! He discovers and recognizes that something within us that makes us special and from that day on, my colt and my service to Him became that something. My colt now was special, not because it had never been ridden, but because of who had ridden it and the purpose of that day. It was on my colt that the Master made His triumphant ride into Jerusalem that Passover!

"I am special because you have made me so, Master... Amen."

The Bystander and the Widow's Mite

Sacrificial Giving

Luke 21:1-4

"Joseph! Joseph of Arimathea… Joseph!" I got up and greeted him. I asked him where he was going and he said he was looking for Nicodemus. Did I know Nicodemus? "Yes, yes," I replied. "Everyone knows both of you. He's right over there." We walked over to him together. They invited me to join them for some refreshment, but I had to say no. I was waiting for the Master, who had asked me to meet Him here today. He had been most insistent on this specific time, so I didn't want to miss our appointment. "Oh," they said with a small smile and walked away.

My name (or what people call me) is the Rich Ruler. I have a real name, you know, but most people would rather define me by what I am than who I am. I've often wondered why people do that… they seem to find it easier to place people in categories rather than get to know them as individuals. I guess I may be a bit like that myself. It was part of the reason I wanted to talk to Him again. So, there I sat, waiting for the Master.

Joseph of Arimathea and Nicodemus… imagine meeting them here! Both are men of tremendous stature in Jerusalem. They both serve in the Sanhedrin. When asked questions of faith they always simply say, "I am seeking the Kingdom of God." Their sincerity and devotion are above reproach. Even Pilate holds them in high regard.

I watched them as they walked away. After words of prayer, they very discreetly made their way to the collection receptacles which resembled horns to make their offerings and then left. As I watched them, it occurred to me that these two men are some of the wealthiest in all of Palestine. And yet, I know they are followers of Jesus. *So why*, I asked myself, *did they get to keep their money when He had asked me to give all of mine away?* Another point to discuss with the Master.

And so I waited in the Temple built by Herod the Great, a masterpiece of architectural achievement and the third Temple to be built on this site. Solomon the "Wise" built the first Temple, but to say this one was built by Herod the "Great" is debatable. While he was certainly responsible for rebuilding God's house, along with amphitheaters, ports, palaces and extensive works around Jerusalem… a massive building campaign designed to show his power… his home life was an offense to God. He murdered his father-in-law, several wives and two sons. His invited guests were enjoying themselves in his lavish swimming pool when he ordered his guards to drown them all. He was an evil and corrupt (and quite possibly mad) man.

There were actually three temples built on this site. King Solomon built the first temple, which was burned by King Nebuchadnezzar. Zerubbabel built the second temple after Cyrus II allowed the Jews to return to Jerusalem. It was always considered "substandard", although it lasted 495 years until Herod decided to rebuild it as part of his construction program.

This Temple has a series of concentric courts. At the center is the Holy of Holies, entered only one time each year on the Day of Atonement. Then there is the Court of the Priests, a Court of Israel, the Court of Women and lastly a Court of Gentiles. The Court of Women is where people make their offerings. The offerings are placed in the thirteen collection boxes which resemble horns… narrow at the top and bell shaped at the bottom.

What a show! I sat there and watched the people make their offerings and couldn't help but notice how more than a few acted, almost like a performance, while making their donations. They first attracted attention to themselves by making exaggerated movements using scripted gestures. With their heads piously bowed, they made certain everyone saw that they put their offering into all thirteen collection boxes. Oohs and ahhs of admiration were heard throughout the courtyard. They were center stage, the main event. Who could love God more or be more righteous?

Amidst all of this piety and ostentatious display, I noticed a poor woman quietly trying to make her offering, undoubtedly intimidated by the value of her gift compared to the offerings of those giving so much. Her offering was just two lepta, the smallest of coins. It is also called a mite. *I know her*, I thought. *Poor woman, life has treated her harshly.* She had lost her husband several years ago to a lingering disease that had gradually paralyzed him to a point where the only things that moved were his eyes. Her entire life for years revolved around caring for him until he died. Then, within months, her two daughters began to show signs of ill health. Within a year, they both died, leaving her completely alone. She subsisted by making bread and selling the loaves in the market. Most thought her tragedies were some kind of punishment sent by God. Indeed, until recently I would have been one of them. Given her circumstances, I was surprised she had anything at all to give.

Remembering what the Rabbi preached, that the poor are beloved of God, I took a deep breath, got up and walked over to her to see if I could assist her in some way. As I shielded her so that she could make her offering without the glare of judging eyes, I looked up and there was the Master, standing where I had been sitting. He was watching me and smiling. Why? I looked down at the widow. She was so tiny and shriveled and thin, bent over from hard labor, dressed in robes that were dusty and tattered. She had deep circles under her eyes and deep wrinkles on her face; she was just about the most pitiful thing I had ever seen. Then she looked up at me and smiled. Her dark brown eyes glowed with happiness and her whole body trembled with the joy she was feeling, joy that she was able to express her love even in this small way. I was filled with amazement… and then shame. I had never felt this joy when depositing an offering, even though my offerings were ten times, no, a hundred times the amount of hers. And then… I got it.

Sacrificial giving should not be evaluated based on the worth of the gift but on the donor's ability to give. Jesus was preaching on this very subject on this particular day. He had been watching the display put on by the wealthy citizens as they theatrically dropped their donations into the horns. He used the example of the widow as a demonstration of His point. Now, to most people in that courtyard, the larger gifts were clearly of greater value, but Jesus said no, the widow's gift was of greater worth because of the circumstances under which it was given.

The widow's gift was almost certainly the smallest offering dropped into the collection box that day. But in Jesus' mind, this poor widow gave the largest gift of all, because she had given everything she had. The others gave out of their abundance… they wanted for nothing as a result of their generosity. She gave out of her poverty. In choosing to give these coins to God, she was undoubtedly choosing not to buy food or some other necessity. She did it because of her sincere love of God, not wanting or expecting any praise for her action.

I realized then what Jesus wanted from me. We all have our different roles to play. I had been given great wealth, power and influence. Jesus wanted me to use those gifts not for my own benefit, but for the benefit of others. My path to heaven was not one of isolation, praying and contemplating the next world while doing nothing to improve this one. I must try to emulate the true devotion of people like this poor widow, gaining admittance into the heavenly kingdom by living a committed life of devotion and dedication on earth. I walked with the widow out of the Temple and took my first steps toward a new life. A life-long journey of giving… giving of my money, my property, myself to those who have less than I. Now, when someone gives sacrificially, I call it "the widow's mite" in honor of that first widow.

Now, I must continue my journey.

"Lord, grant me the clarity of sight to look beyond the frauds, to seek out those who are pure and true of heart and to strive to emulate them in my own life… Amen."

Man with Water Jar

Ready When Needed

Luke 22:7-38

Maybe the man with the colt felt special, but I sure didn't. I seldom made eye contact with anyone. I had the most demeaning job a man in my day could have and the low self-esteem to go with it… fetching water from the well. I was little more than a maid. I had tried to assert myself, but it would always fail. I'd look more foolish than ever. Face it, God made a mistake when he created me. Oh how I prayed each night to be somebody else. Each morning I awakened to the same old me... a shy, unimportant, non-talented water carrier.

Why, I even tried to be a disciple. What a joke. Even the Master didn't want me. The lame, the blind, beggars, harlots… He chose them, but He actually told me to go about my work, that the Lord would call me at the needed time. Now, when the champion of the unloveables didn't want me… well, all hope of changing or doing something important with my life was gone!

One day, I was returning from the well, feeling oh-so-sorry for myself when I noticed two men following me. I quickened my pace and went into the house. I told the steward what had happened. As we spoke, the two men appeared at the door. The master of the home recognized them and greeted them warmly. When they left, he summoned the other servants and announced with great joy that the Master would have Passover there in the upper room. My job was to make sure that there was enough water. Big deal!

That night, God gave to me a privilege afforded to no other. Before our time in that upper room was over and the disciples went out singing after the Seder meal ended, Jesus rose from the table and motioned for me to come and assist Him. He said His time had come. From my jar, He poured the water into a bowl which He used to wash the feet of the disciples. It was such a moving experience. "Not my feet, Lord," Peter pulled his feet away, but Jesus said something then Peter stuck his feet out and Jesus washed Peter's feet.

Jesus then spoke to His disciples, "The greatest among you should be like the youngest, and the one who rules like the one who serves. For who is greater, the one who is at the table or the one who serves? Is it not the one who is at the table? But I am among you as one who serves. You are those who have stood by me in my trials. And I confer on you a kingdom, just as my Father conferred one on me, so that you may eat and drink at my table in my kingdom and sit on thrones, judging the twelve tribes of Israel." *Luke 22:26-30*

I didn't know until later the significance of this. Amazing! I had been called upon to assist in teaching one of Jesus' greatest messages. We all are called not to be served but to serve. Not to be the Master, but the Servant.

You may think that what you are doing is unimportant. You may feel that you are a nobody. Be faithful. Turn it all over to the Master and He will call upon you when needed! Be prepared. No task given to us by the Master is unimportant.

"Keep me, Master, faithful to the job you have given me... Amen."

Judas

Betrayed With a Kiss

Luke 22:47-48

A kiss! The Son of Man betrayed with a kiss. How cruel. How ironic. An expression of love marked me as the executioner!

Things happened so quickly. It all got out of control. How did it all begin? Why? What started it? What's the difference? It's all over now. A kiss! Oh God, not with a kiss!

I did not wish it so. I made a mistake. I listened to the wrong people. And that voice I kept hearing… first a whisper, then louder, louder, until it had complete control over me. I did its bidding. The things I knew were wrong but seemed to be right. As I led them to the garden that night, the voice made me feel strong, heroic. "Your name will be remembered for all the ages," it whispered, "children will sing it in songs of praise. This one act will make you immortal."

The kiss. As my lips touched His cheek, the voice laughed, a triumphant, jeering, horrifying laugh, and spoke to me no more. Instead, my ears were filled with the noise of the arrest. A clash of swords. Cries. Screams. "How could you, Judas?" the other disciples yelled at me while running from the garden. And His words, "Judas, are you betraying the Son of Man with a kiss?" *Luke 22:48*

It wasn't for the money, I swear. I didn't care about the money. I just wanted Him to see that He was hurting our cause by not taking action. I just wanted to force His hand to lead us against the Romans, to drive them from our land. We did not need a Messiah carrying love in His heart but rather a sword in His hand. Many of us were ready to fight.

Oh, God, a kiss! I thought a kiss would tell Him I still loved Him and yet still be a call to action. A call to use His powers more carefully, to use them to save us from the conquering powers of this world. I am repeating myself. I just did not believe that He meant everything He said. A number of times, He said that His kingdom was not of this world. *I did not know that He would die for this!*

Betrayed, yes, but by one who loved Him and whom He loved and... with a kiss.

These lips which betrayed the Son of Man will kiss no other. They will not speak again nor take substance for this body; I will seal them for eternity. They will neither betray nor love another again.

"Master, I am frightened thinking of the capacity for evil within me. Please give me the strength to resist evil, to open myself to your grace and to find the courage to live my life in accordance with your will for me... Amen."

High Priest's Servant

Lose an Ear, Gain Eternal Life

Luke 22:49-51

An innocent bystander! That's what I was. I had been awakened in the middle of the night. I was only to observe and report back to the High Priest. I didn't know anything, only that I just wanted it to be over so I could go back to bed. We arrived at the garden called Gethsemane. Then before I knew it, a fight broke out. A sword struck me on my head. I thought I was going to die! Blood was everywhere. "Oh God, no!" I screamed as I fell to the ground. Then the fighting really began. The guards drew their swords and charged the Rabbi and His followers. It would be ended there and then.

With a weary, but powerful voice, the Rabbi called for it all to end. Everyone stopped immediately. His disciples were puzzled that He had called them from His defense; the Temple guards seemed, for the moment, to have lost the will to fight. Even then the Galilean had power over others. The wind, sea, and even these hardened soldiers obeyed him.

He then directed his attention toward me. I was bleeding heavily. I could not tell where I was cut. I heard someone say that it was my ear. It had almost been severed. The Rabbi took a cloth from around his waist and put it to the bleeding wound. Then, He touched my wound with His hands. The bleeding and pain stopped. As they led Him away, I saw His hands tied behind Him. They were stained with my blood.

I went to my room and washed off the blood. Some friends examined my wound. My ear was reattached… I was completely healed! I was so exhausted and confused, I drank a large cup of wine and eventually fell to sleep. When I awoke the next morning, I had a strong desire to see the Master again. I was touched by His compassion. Knowing He was probably being taken to His death, He stopped to care for me. He was everything people said about Him. I had never felt such love before.

When I got there, it was too late. There before me He hung upon the cross. I looked at His hands… hands stained with His blood and mine. In healing me, my blood had stained His hands; in saving me, His blood had removed the stain of sin from my life. The night I met the Master I lost an ear but with the Master's compassion, I not only regained my ear but gained my soul.

"Master, come into my life when I least expect it... bring healing and love... Amen."

The Maid

When the Cock Crowed

Luke 22:54-62

We knew it was him. All three of us recognized him. We had built a fire in the courtyard that night. We didn't want to miss any of the action. As we were sitting around the fire telling what we knew and taking bets on the outcome, the big one, who had the smell of salt water and fish about him, came and sat by us. He tried to hide his face, but we knew who he was. My statement brought a denial. Then a little later another said the same to him, but again he denied ever knowing the Galilean. And then just about daybreak… yes, I remember it so clearly… a third time someone named him and he denied it again. A cock crowed, and there before us in the doorway was the Rabbi. As the guards led Him past us He looked down at this man. When the Rabbi was gone, His friend, whom we had known all along to be His disciple, lowered his head and began to weep bitterly.

The others left… just the two of us remained. The excitement we anticipated never materialized. It was cold and damp. The hours ahead promised more of the same. The fire was all but gone. And somehow, the sight of a big strong man crying, well, it touched me. Did the Rabbi actually mean this much to him? Perhaps, but I don't think that was it… I think it was what he did. But what did he do that was so terrible? He just denied knowing Him. What was the big deal? He was frightened, so he lied. We were just two nobodies… a serving maid and a fisherman, not like the poor Rabbi. It wasn't like a court of law. Besides, what would it have gained him or the Galilean if he confessed to the world that he knew Him? The fisherman was of no consequence. They had the one they wanted. Why then, was he so upset?

Then it hit me. He had let the Rabbi down. I guess when the Rabbi needed him, he wasn't there for Him. The Rabbi was disheartened, the fisherman ashamed. I don't know… there was something more there than I will ever understand. But what was it? What made these people so attached to this man? Even when it was hopeless they still stayed around. It was as if they were waiting for something to happen… something more than His death, which would surely come. I couldn't figure it out.

But what I did know, what I could see right there in front of me, was that none of them had been or ever would be the same since they met this man they called the Master.

"In meeting you Master, I too, will never be the same. May this change in me make a change in the world around me… Amen."

Pilate

Remembered For All Time

Luke 23:1-7, 13-25

In your time, so I'm told, people say that I'd only be a footnote in history if fate had not placed me in Jerusalem on that night. Because of it I'm famous, or should I say, infamous. How does one of your creeds go "... and crucified under Pontius Pilate?" True, but not true. It wasn't me, but you. That's right... you!

Don't plead the innocence of time. You were there as surely as I was, maybe not in the flesh, but in the spirit... the human spirit. That is what crucified Him. We were all participants; I merely had a leading role. Sound crazy? You think I'm trying to find a scapegoat? Think of it. Am I not correct? You can't lay it all on me! I am as innocent as you... or as guilty... however you want to look at it.

They got me out of bed in the middle of the night. I was incredibly annoyed. What was so important it couldn't wait until morning? Then I saw Him and I understood... it was the Galilean... the one they had been grumbling about and plotting against for months. They had finally trapped Him somehow and wanted to take action before His followers somehow freed Him. They began to make accusations against Him... an insurrectionist, they said, telling people they shouldn't pay taxes and that they should rise up with a sword and drive the Romans out. He had been claiming to be God, they said, King of the Jews, so He was a traitor as well... an enemy of Caesar.

I just rolled my eyes at these allegations. It was obvious what they were doing... they wanted me to do what they were not allowed... to find Him guilty and execute Him.

In the blink of an eye, this whole Hebrew mess was placed in my lap. I had to maintain a cool head; this was simply another legal matter to be settled. That was my job, remember! Keep the peace. Keep the Hebrews happy taxpayers. I didn't want to condemn Him, but the Pharisees were going to cause trouble if I didn't do something, and they were the ones who controlled the Hebrews.

Simply put, this Rabbi of yours would not give me anything with which to work. Sensing that this might be a religious matter, I tried to give Him a way out. I asked Him point blank if He was the King of the Jews and He just shrugged His shoulders and said, "You have said so." *Luke 23:3*

What was I supposed to do with that? Three times I tried to call off this crucifixion but each time the Hebrew leaders shouted even louder, "Crucify him!" I didn't want to do it, but my hands were tied just as firmly as were His. I had no choice. I didn't order Him to be crucified, I simply allowed things to happen. I listened to the will of the people.

I suppose if there is any guilt on my part, and I have often thought of that day, it was allowing this to happen at all. I could have stopped it. I will never forget that day I met this Master of yours. I will never forget that I could have stopped it... maybe... but maybe not. Besides, I enjoyed sending Him back to my old "friend" Herod Antipas, the Tetrarch over Galilee, who just happened to be in Jerusalem. I always loved to see him squirm. *Let him make the call.*

"Master, may duty never become more important than love... Amen."

Herod

Like Father, Like Son

Luke 23:8-12

You've heard a lot about me. Well, meet me now in person! I'm Herod. You know, the bad guy. I murdered John and had a part in your "Master's" demise. Circumstances! That's right, I was a victim of circumstances, especially with the Galilean. John was another matter. Face it… it was either him or me. I had to act with authority or I'd have looked like a fool in front of that grubby peasant. Nothing should have happened to John, that pesky fly. I tried to shoo him away but, no, he kept buzzing in my face. His bites were small but irritating. I didn't set out to kill him. He simply was at the wrong place at the wrong time. I was drunk... oh, never mind.

It's the Rabbi we're talking about, right? He was one of my very own subjects, a Galilean. Pilate became my "friend" that day by showing me the "respect" of allowing me to decide the fate of one of my own subjects. I really appreciated that and I told Pilate so at the next party. That snake in the grass… he did that hoping I'd get in trouble.

Where was I? Oh yes, Jesus. How pleased I was to see this Jesus. I had heard so much about Him. I would have given anything to see one of His famous miracles (especially the changing-the-water-into-wine… that could be really useful). I was prepared to kill one of my slaves so that Jesus could raise him from the dead, but nothing. He just stood there and stared at me. Listen, I could have greatly helped His career. But no, He was too much into this martyr role. And did He speak a word to me? No. No words. No miracles. Well, finally the priests and lawyers showed up. Were they ever livid! The entertainment was over. I had to get tough. I didn't want these religious fanatics turning on me. Oh, I could have squashed them like insects, but that wouldn't have been a wise choice politically. We didn't want any more trouble around there than we already had.

I did what I had to do. I played the game. I treated Him with contempt and ridicule and sent Him back to Pilate with my compliments. Listen, He had it coming. What was I to do? He wouldn't even speak up in His own defense. Besides, He didn't please me. A little miracle, that's all I wanted. Was that too much to ask?

Oh, by the way, how is this for irony? It was my father, Herod the Great, who tried to find and kill Jesus when He was a baby just born in Bethlehem. Now I, as his son, some 34 years later, helped kill Jesus as a man.

Meeting your Master was such a bore!

"It's difficult to believe that there is such evil as this in the world. Master, keep such evil from my heart and my house... Amen."

Simon of Cyrene

A Cross to Bear

Luke 23:26

Have you ever had something pushed on you, something you didn't want? Well, that's exactly what happened to me the day I met the Master. I was just passing through Jerusalem when I heard all the commotion. Out of curiosity, I stood on the side of the street with the others. I had never seen a crucifixion before and I really didn't want to see one now. A glimpse at those traveling to the hill was enough to satisfy my curiosity.

I admit, I wanted to get a look at this Galilean about whom everyone was talking. At night, when I checked into the inn, and again as I was leaving in the morning, every conversation centered on this man. From what I could gather, the people felt that He hadn't merited such a punishment.

He simply was a small town boy who had gotten caught up in big city politics. Still, one man in the crowd impressed me with what he said of the Galilean. He told of things the man was supposed to have done… healing the sick, raising the dead. Of course, I'd have to see that to believe it. But he also spoke of His love for the poor, the helpless, the unloveable. That struck home. Why would a man sacrifice his life for those kinds of people? To die for the spoils of a city, the riches of a kingdom, yes! But for people like me? I felt compelled to at least go to see Him. I didn't want to get in any trouble. I didn't belong there. I just wanted to see Him for a few seconds and then be on my way, as something to tell my grandchildren.

I heard the whip crack. The cries of those lining the streets became louder and louder. The Galilean was coming closer. He was in front of me. He fell to the ground, and His cross fell on top of Him. I became sick to my stomach at the sight of this man… injured, bleeding and bruised. A crown of thorns was pressed into His scalp. Why had I come? As I was pushing and shoving, trying to make my way back from the crowd, a Roman soldier grabbed me by the arm. "You," he said, "carry the cross…. hurry this thing along." Within the span of a few seconds I was in the procession. I was carrying the cross of the Galilean. He spoke not a word to me, although His hand often rested on my back. Blood was in His eyes. He could not see to walk. His breathing was labored, His face bruised from the beating and bloody lashings covered His body.

When we reached the hill called Golgotha, which means "Place of the Skull," they took the cross from me and pushed me aside. I watched as they crucified Him. I vomited. I wanted to leave, but I stayed. I stayed until He died. I heard all He said. Somehow I knew He had died for me and He did not even know my name. He loved me even though a word from His lips never was spoken to me. All that He had ever said, all that He had ever done, His death said it all in one perfect deed. I had met the Master, His blood was upon me, the blood He shed for me and you.

"Master, may I each day help carry your cross. Give me the strength to do so…
Amen."

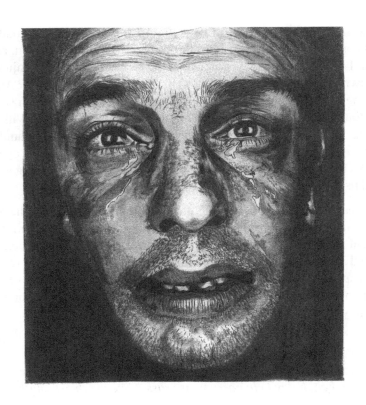

Criminal

It's Never Too Late

Luke 23:32-43

I have… but a few minutes… to live. This hellish night... nightmare will soon... be over. I am past pain now... I am drifting... in and out... But I can't die without telling... without telling you of something important. Life is more than what is… is seen. I have seen it all. I have done it all, and… I am receiving what… is coming to me. But when you see this man die for… doing good… for loving others… then either He is madder than I… or… worse yet… more evil, because He's leading others to their senseless death or… He has come from God to save us… and… this… I believe is the truth.

The Centurion called out that it is three… three o'clock… the Rabbi has been on the cross… for three hours. Why did they… hate Him so? They used nails too… they wanted the Rabbi to die quickly. My partner and I… well, they wanted us to… die a slow and painful death… our crimes… crimes were many. How can they crucify a Rabbi… espec… especially this one… a man who said we… we should love one another.

Look at the crowd surrounding us… the only ones here are the victims of… of… of our crimes. They… they came to throw stones… spit at… us and curse us. The Rabbi has… also drawn a large crowd. Many have come… to see Him suffer… and die. They seem to be… getting a sadistic pleasure watching Him… Him die. And yet, there is fear in their faces… what power does He still possess? He is dying… His life all but gone… what could this man do? Do they… think the Rabbi has… an army that will come… and rescue Him? Look at His army… a few women looking from afar, a… wo… man and a young boy weeping bitterly at the foot of the cross and several of those "disciples" of His…. My partner, the other thief, is still defiant, yelling at everyone… including the Rabbi. For all the crimes we committed… he was always the victim.

Listen… listen… the Rabbi speaks. I can barely hear His words, He is so weak and His whisper so faint. He says, **"Father, forgive them, for they do not know what they are doing."** *Luke 23:34* He is dying and yet… yet His heart is… not filled with bitterness… but love… and forgiveness.

"Master… Master… Rabbi… Rabbi… " He slowly turns His head, looking at me. "Remember me when you come into your... your kingdom," I begged Him. *Luke 23:42*

He says, "Truly I tell you, today you will be with me in paradise." *Luke 23:43*

I have a choice. My partner in crime chose… chose… death. I have chosen life. And because of that… because… I met the Master on this… my last day of life… I have been invited to be… with Him in His… kingdom. Praise God! What I looked for in living… I have found in dying… with Him.

He gasps and says, "It is finished." *John 19:30* And He dies… He dies… He died…

They are taking the Rabbi down and carrying Him away. My partner has died… I am the last to come down. Today… I will… be with… the Rabbi in…

"Oh Lord… may we always remember it is never too late… Amen."

Joseph of Arimathea

A Secret Disciple No Longer

Luke 23:50-56

I came from a little town nestled in the foothills of Judea called Arimathea. I decided one day to relocate my profitable business and move my family to Jerusalem. I purchased enough property to accommodate my growing family and expanding business. What drew me to this parcel of land was its location, together with a beautiful little garden and a family tomb cut from limestone. It had never been used. This is where generations after generations of my family would be put to rest.

Under Roman occupation, we all had to be careful as to what we said and did. I hated politics and the social unrest that came with it. It was bad for business. It was obvious I was not political… quite the contrary. People no longer said "Joseph of Arimathea," but "Joseph, the one searching for the Kingdom of God."

One day, I was approached by a few of the members of the ruling council called the Sanhedrin. They wanted me to become a member. *Too much politics*, I thought, but I said yes, because declining would be making a political statement. The Romans didn't care about our politics anyway; all they wanted was peace and taxes. The Sanhedrin had power over all the affairs of the Hebrew people, except for the power of the sword. The Council could sentence a man to death, but the Romans had to carry out the execution. The Romans did permit it (or look the other way) for religious crimes or when a mob would stone a woman who committed adultery.

I developed a deep friendship while serving on the Council with a man named Nicodemus. He was such a godly man. He, too, was looking for the Kingdom of God. He was the one who secretly introduced me to the Master. I was reluctant at first, but finally agreed to meet Him. All night long we talked with the young Rabbi from Galilee. We asked Him question after question. I had never heard such answers. We left at first light. We still thought it best to keep things quiet. *Keep things quiet!* We simply were afraid of coming out openly and supporting this courageous Galilean.

I am not sure why the physician included me in his story unless it was because I offered to give Him a decent burial. Taking Him down from the cross and putting His lifeless body in my tomb was not courageous or noble; it was done out of respect and shame. Shame for the way I had acted, especially in those last days and last hours. I was confused. I didn't really know what to do. I loved the Master but I had been raised under the Law. He challenged so many things I had been taught, so much of the way I lived. There was always a shadow of doubt. I just couldn't make the break.

But I never dreamed it would come to this. Yes, I knew the Council felt threatened, angry, but never to the point of killing him. I thought there were enough members, wise men, to prevent good and just men from becoming Satan's tools (and Satan used them so cunningly).

They assembled hastily in the middle of the night, which was unprecedented for the Council. I protested. I made speeches. I called upon old friendships. I pleaded. I demanded. I argued. But I always stopped short of saying I was His disciple. *Disciple?* I would gladly say it now, but who would care? He's dead. This young Rabbi, who came down from Galilee, who passed through my town one day when He was just beginning His ministry, who gathered a crowd about Him and began to preach, who struck up a friendship with me. I never heard anyone preach or teach like He did... and never will again. Nor have I seen anyone do the things He did... heal the sick, give sight to the blind, raise the dead.

That is why I went to Pilate and took His body down and laid Him in my family tomb. I did not care now who knew that I was His disciple. I did for Him in death what I should have done in life... I served Him. God forgive me.

The stone was rolled into place. I, too, met the Master, and I laid Him to rest. I pray to God that I shall one day meet Him again.

"Not a secret follower, Master, but one who will stand up and be known to all as your disciple... Amen."

The Women Who Supported Jesus' Ministry

Always There

Luke 23:49, 24:9-10

In our day, it was terribly frowned upon for men and women to travel together unless they were relatives. Certainly married men did not travel with unmarried women. There was much whispering at the time about Jesus allowing women to follow Him. In time, any talk went away. People could easily see that we had extraordinary love for the Master and for one another. There were never any sexual overtones to our relationship. Quite the contrary, we observed all the rules of the Law for men and women in such an arrangement. When we were travelling with the Master and His disciples, we slept separately, though one of the disciples kept a watch over us all night. We followed all the rules of eating, staying clean, and if possible, we worshiped on the Sabbath in the synagogue.

The twelve Apostles stayed with the Master all the time unless they were needed at home. The disciples came and went. Often, the wives of the married disciples would join us. All along the way, the women would go ahead to the next village and prepare food for the Master and those following Him. We paid all the expenses so the Master and His disciples could fully concentrate on spreading the Good News.

As women, we were greatly restricted in many aspects of everyday life. We learned to be resourceful. Our greatest strength was bonding with other women and the Master. It was unheard of for someone like Jesus, a charismatic Rabbi, to include women in His ministry, even when the women did the work assigned to them by society and the Lord, such as cooking the meals. Jesus insisted that women were equal to men and were to be treated as such. Many of the women followed Jesus because of His kindness towards them, and because He made them feel important in the eyes of God.

"Lord, no matter my gender, intelligence, position or wealth, you see me as a unique, irreplaceable child of God. Please Lord, help me to see others with your clear eyes and to cherish each person I meet as a precious gift from you... Amen."

No Name Disciple

Going to Emmaus

Luke 24:13-35

What a glorious morning. Praise the Lord! I pray this day that you will meet the Master: The Resurrected Lord!

I know what you are thinking: *Who is this man, anyway? Why does Luke not name him? He names his fellow disciple, Cleopas. Why are the two of them not mentioned or referred to in the previous chapters? Why do they now appear? One named Cleopas and the other ("no name"), walking to a place that not even the scholars know much about... a small town named Emmaus. And for what reason?*

Why does Luke tell us of their encounter with the risen Lord? What is so special about them or their story? Surely there were more important, more exciting things that the Master did than meet and break bread with Cleopas and this "no name" disciple? Back to the original question, who is this disciple Luke does not name?

I knew it. You have so many questions. Let me tell you who I am and I believe that will answer all your other questions.

I am... well, perhaps I am... or maybe just possibly, I am... YOU!

My name could be your name. My story, your story. My life, your life. My meeting the Master, your meeting the Master. Luke left me unnamed so that his story of the Master would never be complete until the last one to meet the Master is named. He has extended to you the offer to name me. Possibly, to give me your name. To know the experience of walking with the resurrected Master. To have Him enter your home and to break bread with Him. To have Him open up the Scriptures to you. To experience personally His power and glory in your life. To be called and known to others as His disciple. To be the one who tells one and all, "I have met the Master and He is Lord and Savior of my life." Won't you come and meet him for yourself?

"May this day break forth with joy because I will walk with the Master today and all the days of my life... because... this disciple is me... Amen."